Best of Graphis
EDITORIAL

PAGE ONE PUBLISHING

In the case of some of the reproductions in this book it proved impossible to locate the originals, despite careful research. They were, however, considered to be of such importance that the decision was taken by the present publisher to reproduce from other published sources.

Cover Photographer: Hartwig Klappert

© 1993 by Graphis Press Corp., Dufourstrasse 107, CH-8008 Zürich, Switzerland

© 1993 for this edition by Page One Publishing Pte Ltd, Singapore
Distributed worldwide by Könemann Verlagsgesellschaft mbH, Bonner Str. 126, D-50968 Köln

Designed by Peter Feierabend, Berlin
Text: Hans Heiermann, Cologne
English translation: Michael Hulse, Cologne
French translation: Michèle Schreyer, Cologne

Printed in Singapore
ISBN 981-00-4771-1

Foreword

The magazines of the Sixties and Seventies tend to bring a rueful smile to our lips nowadays. In those bygone days before the advent of desktop publishing, the designs dreamt up by the unbridled imaginations of art directors and lay-out specialists were still shackled by the costs incurred at the graphic design and type-setting stages. Nowadays, though, publishers everywhere have invested in the inevitable hardware and software, and design work is done at the click of the mouse. Given the enormous range of design options now available, content is losing in importance. The main thing is stylish excellence in the presentation. The prevalence of desktop publishing (DTP) constitutes a milestone on the print media's bright and beautiful way to zero information content.

DTP may sound to the layman like a pesticide – an impression which may not be so very absurd. The new visual technology has meant significant progress "in heaving off the burden of language and destroying everything that once went by the name of programming, meaning or content". Hans Magnus Enzensberger's critique of television can be easily transferred to magazines, the glossy showcase of editorial design.

To say this is not to lament the fact, nor to grind the axe of culture criticism. Those who make use of the media get what they are prepared to pay for, and what they want: "Far from being manipulated (educated, informed, warned, enlightened, instructed) by the medium, they use it to fulfil their wishes. If their wishes do not prevail, they punch the button to withdraw their affection. If they do, they reward the medium with high viewing rates." Thus it is with television. And in the print media the same process operates in terms of purchase or not.

Magazines are there to be leafed through and put aside. They require a minimum of concentration and are like luxury consumer goods in creating continuing demand for themselves. Editorial design is content without meaning, smartly done up to use combinations of pictures and type so that words become decorative and text merely a component in a visual look. Editorial design is advertising – for itself and itself alone.

Advertising and editorial design are accomplices in the self-same lifestyle aesthetic, and in many magazines they have become impossible to distinguish. Taken together, they still assure the colourful mix that is sometimes mistaken for diversity of programme – truthfully enough, if mere assertion constitutes a programme.

Where on earth does the irresistible appeal of these minimal-meaning media come from? Why are they so successful? Enzensberger sees them as a kind of "auto-medication". In his view, they are "the only universal form of psychotherapy available on a mass scale". Their impact derives from the pleasure people plainly take in switching off. Seen in these terms, magazines and the editorial design that underwrites their success deserve to be considered as an important contribution to the general well-being.

Power to the therapists! And (of course) we hope you enjoy this book.

Vorwort

Wer heute Illustrierte und Magazine der sechziger und siebziger Jahre durchblättert, wird sich eines wehmütigen Lächelns über ihr Design nicht ganz erwehren können. In diesen prä-DTP-historischen Zeiten war die ausschweifende Phantasie der Artdirectors und Layouter noch an die Kostenkette von Grafikern und Satzstudios gelegt. Inzwischen haben alle Verlage in die unumgängliche Hard- und Software investiert, und es wird wie entfesselt per Mausklick gestaltet. Angesichts der enormen Designmöglichkeiten verlieren Themen und Inhalte immer mehr an Bedeutung, Hauptsache, sie werden exzellent aufgemacht und gut gestylt präsentiert. Die Verbreitung des Desktop Publishing ist ein Meilenstein auf dem Weg der bunten Printmedien zur Nullinformation und totalen Zerstreuung.

Bei DTP denkt der Laie vermutlich an ein Schädlingsbekämpfungsmittel. Ganz unsinnig ist die Vorstellung übrigens nicht: Mit den neuen visuellen Techniken ist man ein beachtliches Stück weitergekommen, „die Last der Sprache wirklich abzuwerfen und alles, was einst Programm, Bedeutung, ‚Inhalt‘ hieß, zu liquidieren". Was Hans Magnus Enzensberger hier mit Blick auf das Fernsehen sagt, läßt sich ohne weiteres auf Illustrierte und Magazine, die Prunkstücke des Editorial Designs, übertragen.

Diese Feststellungen werden hier keineswegs lamentierend und in kulturkritischer Absicht vorgetragen. Der Nutzer der Medien erhält, wofür er zu zahlen bereit ist und was er sich folglich so und nicht anders wünscht: „Weit davon entfernt, sich manipulieren (erziehen, informieren, bilden, aufklären, mahnen) zu lassen, manipuliert er das Medium, um seine Wünsche durchzusetzen. Wer sich ihnen nicht fügt, wird per Tastendruck mit Liebesentzug bestraft, wer sie erfüllt, durch herrliche Quoten belohnt." So ist es beim Fernsehen, bei den Printmedien funktioniert der gleiche Mechanismus über den Kauf oder seine Verweigerung.

Illustrierte und Magazine sind dazu da, durchgeblättert und zur Seite gelegt zu werden. Sie erfordern ein Minimum an Aufmerksamkeit und wirken wie Genußmittel, die immer neues Verlangen erzeugen. Editorial Design ist die schmucke Form sinnentleerter Inhalte: die variantenreiche Kombination von Bildern und Typographie, bei der die Schrift zum Ornament, der Text zum beliebigen Gegenstand der Gestaltung wird. Editorial Design ist tendenziell Werbung für – nichts, außer für sich selbst. Werbung und Editorial Design sind Komplizen der gleichen Lifestyle-Ästhetik und in vielen Blättern kaum noch zu unterscheiden. Gemeinsam garantieren sie jene bunte Mischung, die manche immer noch für Programmvielfalt halten. Versteht man „Programm" als bloße Ankündigung, ist dem nicht zu widersprechen.

Was in aller Welt macht den unwiderstehlichen Reiz dieser Minimalsinn-Medien aus? Worin ist ihr Erfolg begründet? Enzensberger hält sie für eine Art der „Selbstmedikation" und „die einzige universelle und massenhaft verbreitete Form der Psychotherapie". Ihre Wirkung liegt in der – offensichtlich lustvollen – Zerstreuung. In diesem Sinn müssen Illustrierte und Magazine und der Garant ihres Erfolgs, das Editorial Design, als wichtiger Beitrag zur allgemeinen Volksgesundheit begriffen werden.

Alle Macht den Therapeuten! Und natürlich: viel Spaß beim Blättern!

Préface

Celui qui feuillette aujourd'hui des illustrés et des magazines des années 60 et 70 ne pourra s'empêcher de sourire avec nostalgie en considérant leur style. En ces temps historiques pré-DTP la fantaisie des directeurs artistiques et dessinateurs était encore tenue en laisse par l'aspect financier que représentaient les graphistes et les ateliers de composition. Aujourd'hui tous les éditeurs ont investi dans les matériels et logiciels informatiques devenus incontournables, et le clic de la souris dispose et compose. Face aux énormes possibilités de design les thèmes et les contenus deviennent de plus en plus anodins. Le principal est qu'ils soient bien apprêtés et que leur présentation soit bien conçue. La diffusion du Desktop Publishing est un jalon sur la voie des médias imprimés en couleur vers l'information zéro et le divertissement à l'état pur.

Le mot DTP évoque probablement pour le profane un produit insecticide, et la comparaison n'est pas si stupide qu'on pourrait le penser: les nouvelles techniques ont permis de franchir un pas considérable, de «vraiment jeter par dessus-bord le poids de la langue et de liquider tout ce qui signifiait autrefois programme, signification, contenu». Ce que dit ici Hans Enzensberger en parlant de la télévision, est également vrai pour les illustrés et les magazines, avec lesquels l'Editorial Design se fait valoir.

Il n'est nullement question ici de se lamenter ou de critiquer la culture. Celui qui utilise les médias reçoit ce pourquoi il est prêt à payer et donc ce qu'il désire comme ceci et pas autrement: «Bien loin de se laisser manipuler (instruire, informer, cultiver, éclairer, avertir), il manipule les médias pour arriver à ses fins. Il lui suffit d'appuyer sur un bouton pour châtier celui qui ne se plie pas à ses désirs en lui prodiguant moins d'amour et pour récompenser ceux qui le font par une audience record.» Le mécanisme est le même en ce qui concerne les médias imprimés: ici on achète ou on refuse d'acheter.

Les illustrés et les magazines sont là pour être feuilletés et mis de côté. Ils exigent un minimum d'attention, leur action est comparable à celles des stimulants, qui engendrent toujours plus de besoin. L'Editorial Design est la forme pimpante de contenus vidés de leur sens: la combinaison riche en images et caractères variés, par laquelle l'écriture devient ornement, le texte un objet quelconque servant à la mise en forme. L'Editorial Design est une publicité tendancieuse pour – rien, excepté pour lui-même. La publicité et l'Editorial Design sont complices de la même esthétique Lifestyle et on a peine à les distinguer l'un de l'autre dans de nombreux journaux. Ensemble ils garantissent ce mélange multicolore que d'aucuns considèrent encore comme une multiplicité des programmes. Si l'on comprend le mot «programme» comme un simple écrit pour annoncer ce qui va venir, on ne peut les contredire.

Mais qu'est-ce-qui peut bien faire le charme irrésistible de ces médias sans réelle signification? Sur quoi est fondé leur succès? Enzensberger les considère comme une sorte d'«automédication» et comme «l'unique forme de psychothérapie universelle et diffusée massivement». Son efficacité est fondée sur la distraction manifestement plaisante qu'elle propose. En ce sens les illustrés et les magazines, et celui à qui ils doivent leur succès, l'Editorial Design, doivent être compris comme une contribution importante à la santé populaire.

Les thérapeutes au pouvoir! Et naturellement, amusez-vous bien en feuilletant cet album.

Client
Elle Magazine
Art Director
Clive Crook
Designer
Debi Angel
Photographer
James Johnson
Editor
Charlotte Du Cann
Typographer
John Bullard-O'Sullivan

A SENSE OF ORDER

Amid stark white walls and highly polished oak floors, four Jacob chairs, an Egyptian Revival chaise and a large white cube appear like vignettes in a still life. These objects, though few in number, have been arranged with utmost precision.

"My last apartment was even sparer," recalls Robert L. Turner, creative director of In Fashion, a television production company. "It was a studio on the 29th floor with black lacquered walls, 28 feet of glass and only a bed in the middle of the room. I felt as though I were living in a jewel box in the sky." This apartment has something of a jewel-like quality, too. Unlike the modernists of 20 years ago, Turner has used minimalist ideas in a romantic fashion.

So has Suzie Frankfurt, a longtime friend of Turner's and the New York-based decorator who collaborated with him on the renovation of this two-bedroom apartment. "We worked hand in hand," says Turner. "The apartment hadn't been touched for over 30 years. With mustard-green walls and antiquated kitchen appliances, the place looked like a set from 'The Honeymooners.'"

Turner's penchant for simplicity, he says, is a reaction to his parents' cluttered home in Baton Rouge, La. Frankfurt's vision stems from an effort to find some relief from the oppressive, often trivial-minded designs that are a result of the recent craze among decorators for re-creating the Belle Epoque. While Frankfurt herself lives in a Regency Revival town house resplendent with ornate Biedermeier furniture, she feels design is on the brink of change. "Things have just become too claustrophobic," the designer says. "That doesn't mean I'm going to put modern furniture in a modern environment. But if you study the great homes of 18th-century Europe, they have an orderliness about them that's much to be admired."

Here, orderliness was achieved by removing a wall to combine the living and dining rooms, off of which is the all-white newly renovated kitchen. And while the walls are devoid of such details as moldings or baseboards, the designer created an octagonal entrance hall that features a pair of black glass columns punctuated by century-old Corinthian capitals and bases.

By studying the original floor plans, the designer discovered a chimney flue that had been blocked. She had it opened up and had a Louis XVI marble mantel installed, now the central focus of the bedroom. For proximity to the fireplace, the bed floats in the middle of the space. Beside it is a méridienne, an Empire love seat with one arm higher than the other, one of a matched pair found at auction.

The second méridienne, draped in a paisley shawl, can be found in the library, originally the second bedroom. This room, with its purple glazed walls, marbleized bookshelves and Audubon prints, is a departure from the rooms in the rest of the apartment. "Everything I'm not sure what to do with always ends up here," Turner says. But still a sense of order pervades.

A white cube, a Louis XVI Jacob chair and a painting by the Italian artist Carlo Maria Mariani all are arranged like a still life.

LIZZIE HIMMEL

Art Director
Susan Slover
Designer
Mario Pulice / Susan Slover
Photographer
Lizzie Himmel
Agency
Susan Slover Design
Publisher
The New York Times

SOTTO LA LUNA

Sotto la luna a tirar tardi per il piacere di tirar tardi si diceva una volta. O per portare avanti una «occasione sentimentale», come invece direbbe un ragazzo di oggi. Per provare un brivido lungo la schiena mentre i passi risuonano sull'acciottolato, come scriverebbero Fruttero & Lucentini. Per schiarirsi finalmente le idee all'aria fresca della notte se i pensieri non fanno dormire, come penserebbe una malata di stress. Per andare a una cena all'aperto con gli amici, «un abito dalla scollatura a tuffo dietro, un velo per coprire le spalle» come troverete nella didascalia di una foto di Vogue. Noi aggiungiamo «... e per sentirsi magicamente belle». La luna che passa attraverso i capelli li fa brillare e, se per caso poche ore prima li avrete trattati con quell'Azurée Hair Program di Estée Lauder che è un metodo modernissimo per il fai da te dei capelli, ecco che sembreranno anche una massa incredibilmente folta...

ESTÉE LAUDER Azurée Hair Care Program si compone di otto prodotti, tutti a base di alghe marine e vitamine che lavorano in sinergia. Ci sono tre shampoo tra cui scegliere il proprio, un conditioner nutriente, due spray, una mousse e un impacco per dare lucentezza e corposità.

270

bellezza

accessori ultimissime

Per un'estate colorata. Di MONTORFANO il secchiello plastificato verde con riporti in cuoio naturale traforato. DI PANCALDI il sandalo in pelle multicolore stampata a fiori, con piccola zeppa. DI MARIA CALDERARA le collane folk variopinte.

PIERO GEMELLI

107

Publisher
Condé Nast S.p.A.
Art Director
Alberto Nodolini
Photographer
Piero Gemelli

DIE NEUEN SYMBOLE

eleganz aus Paris: Die neue Herbst-
mode spiegelt die Kreativität der franzö-
sischen Top-Designer – und Symbole bestimmen
ihre wirkungsvolle Optik. Das sind die Kennzeichen der kom-
menden Saison: ein „disziplinierter", doch nicht strenger Look,
mit klaren Konturen. Mit Silhouetten, die den Körper modellie-
ren, und Effekten, die ihn verführerisch in Szene setzen.

EMANUEL UNGARO PARALLÈLE

Paris liebt Eleganz mit Dramatik, wie Samtkappen, Stulpenhand-schuhe, Super-Schmuck. Zur Wolljacke mit Sambesstü gehört ein Glencheck-Rock mit Taft-Plissée (Stoffe: Corisia/Ideacomo-Gruppe). Accessoires von Emanuel Ungaro. Auf allen zwölf Seiten Frisuren: Kim für Mod's Hair, Make-up von Kevyn Aucoin.

138   138

Eric Boman

ERFOLGS-DIÄT

Schlank & schön in sieben Tagen

Delikat essen – und da-
bei abnehmen! Gäste
bewirten und dabei
konsequent Diät halten:
Die neue VOGUE-Diät
bietet alles, was Erfolg
verspricht: Genuß für
Feinschmecker, eine
optimale Versorgung
mit Vitaminen und Mi-
neralstoffen, zeitspa-
rende und effektive
Kochanleitungen. Mit
unserer Erfolgs-Diät
nehmen Sie in sieben
Tagen problemlos drei
Kilo ab. Sie läßt sich gut
um eine Woche verlän-
gern und eignet sich
auch für ein Wochen-
end-Kurzprogramm.

238

VON MARTINA MEUTH

*So funktioniert
die VOGUE-Diät:*

Pro Tag gibt es höchstens 1000 Kalorien. Fest verplant sind davon 200 fürs Früh-stück, je etwa 300 bis 350 für zwei Mahlzeiten: Ein kleineres, oft kaltes Essen, das nicht viel Arbeit macht, und ein etwas aufwendigeres Mahl, zu dem man getrost auch Gäste laden kann (in diesem Fall die im Rezept angegebenen Mengen einfach entsprechend der Anzahl von Mit-Essern vervielfachen). Es bleibt also ein tägliches Guthaben von knapp 200 Kalorien für Extras, falls die Lust auf etwas zum Knabbern zwischendurch oder auf ein Glas Wein doch unüberwindbar wird (siehe Kasten auf Seite 241).

Nach einer Woche zeigt die Waage garantiert fünf bis sechs Pfund weniger. Wer auf die Extra-Kalorien verzichtet, nimmt zur Belohnung schneller und noch mehr ab. Auf gar keinen Fall sollte man aber das Guthaben aufsparen und dann am letzten Tag gesammelt essen.

Die Versorgung mit Vitaminen, Mineral- und Ballaststoffen ist so ausgewogen, daß man die Diät unbesorgt auf zwei, drei Wochen ausdehnen kann. Aber anschließend nur schrittweise und behutsam wieder zu großzügigeren Mahlzeiten zurückkehren, vor allem beim Alkohol maßvoll bleiben, sonst sitzen die endlich verschwundenen Pfunde nur so schnell wieder auf den Hüften. Beschleunigen läßt sich der Erfolg, wenn man die Diätwoche mit folgendem Kur-Drink beginnt: 40 Gramm Glaubersalz (Apotheke) in 3/4 l lauwarmem Wasser auflösen' und in kleinen Schlucken trinken (schmeckt leicht bitter und salzig). Das Abführmittel wirkt schnell, deshalb lieber zu Hause bleiben – die Kur am besten also an einem Wochenende beginnen. Der Körper wird so gründlich entschlackt und aufgeräumt, stellt sich leichter auf die neue Ernährung um und greift freiwilliger und nachhaltiger die eigenen Reserven an.

Wer abnehmen will, muß frühstücken! Auch, wer sonst am Morgen nicht gern etwas zu sich nimmt. Der Magen muß Arbeit bekommen, damit er Sättigung signalisiert. Nur so ist man leistungsfähig und vor der Versuchung gefeit, zu naschen. Man kommt bei einem Frühstück mit nur 200 Kalorien aus. Drei Vorschläge zum Aussuchen und Abwechseln (Seite 241).

Damit der Busen straff bleibt

Während einer Diät ist eine besonders intensive Busenpflege unumgänglich. Der Busen kann durch die Reduzierung des Fettgewebes den „Unterbau" und dadurch auch an Spannkraft verlieren. Mit der neuen „Bust Firming Lotion" von SHISEIDO erzielt man eine Festigung des Hautgewebes. Sie wird täglich nach einer speziellen Methode auf den Busen und auch auf das Dekolleté einmassiert. (Eine bebilderte Massage-Anleitung liegt der Packung bei.) Eine gerade, aufrechte Haltung und Gymnastik kräftigt außerdem den Brustmuskel. Das Kleid auf diesem Foto stammt von John Galliano.

238

Neil Kirk

Publisher
Condé Nast S.p.A.
Art Director
Angelica Blechschmidt
Photographer
Eric Boman

Publisher
Condé Nast S.p.A.
Art Director
Angelica Blechschmidt
Photographer
Neil Kirk

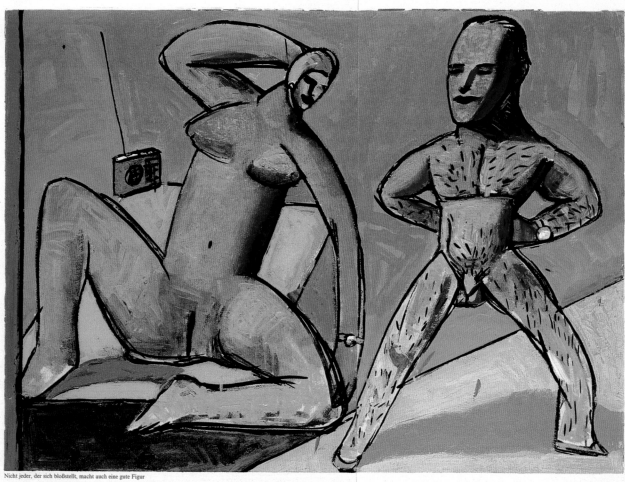

Von Dorothea Friedrich
Illustrationen
Heinz Edelmann

Augen zu und durch! Ach, selten hält der nackte Körper, was der bekleidete versprochen hat. Und nun ist es zu spät. Eine Frage der Höflichkeit. Entblößung liefert aus. Ein solches Angebot zu provozieren und dann auszuschlagen – das hat keiner verdient. Und wer weiß, ob der andere nicht auch enttäuscht ist? Die größte Angst jedes Verliebten beim ersten Auszieben ist die, Widerwillen zu erregen. Nur deshalb tun wir unseren Körpern so viel an. Natürlich wollen wir mit niemandem verwechselt werden. Trotzdem ist es unser Ehrgeiz, anderen so ähnlich wie möglich zu sein. Werden wir dennoch abgelehnt, so können wir wenigstens einen Grund dafür ausschließen. Doch wenn es der Körper nicht war, geht es erst recht an die Substanz. Daran denken wir nicht gleich. Und behaupten doch: Wir wollen um unserer selbst willen geliebt werden!

Lange genug hat abendländische Prüderie den Leib verpönt. Trotzdem: Wir sollten sofort einpacken, wenn wir nicht unmittelbar nach der Preisgabe Lust haben, die eigene Schönheit gelobt zu hören und die fremde Schönheit zu loben. Zwischen Lob und Liebe kann viel Zeit vergehen. Je unaufrichtiger man war, desto länger dauert es. John Fantes Held Arturo Bandini braucht zwei Tage, bis er zu Vera Rivken fährt, die sich gegen seinen Willen vor ihm entkleidet hat, um ihm ihre gräßlichen Narben zu zeigen. Er nennt sie trotzdem wunderschön. Sie gewinnt ihre jungfräuli-

DER NACKTE KÖRPER NACKT

che Scheu zurück, während ihm schlecht wird. Casanova muß als Vorbild herbeizitiert werden, bevor Bandini die Mißgestaltete glücklich machen kann. Er darf die Augen schließen und an seine wahre Geliebte denken. Vera faßt ihn an. Die Melanesier nennen die Augen „Wunsch nach Begattung", doch nach ihrem Sprichwort bleiben nur dem Mann, der die Augen schließt, die Schönheiten der Liebe verborgen. Offensichtlich zieht es die Frau überall vor, sich auf das zu verlassen, was sie ertasten kann, und nicht auf das, was sie sieht.

47

Nicht jeder, der sich bloßstellt, macht auch eine gute Figur

Publication
Frankfurter Allgemeine Magazin
Art Director
Hans-Georg Pospischil
Illustration
Heinz Edelmann

och bevor wir solches erfahren, müssen wir einige Aufregungen hinter uns bringen. Sigmund Freud war noch ganz wohlgemut, als er vom Penisneid der Frauen träumte. Private Überlieferungen schwesterlichen Mitleids mit vermeintlicher brüderlicher Mißgestaltung haben Freud schon früh korrigiert, und René Magritte bestätigt unsere Skepsis: Sein Gestalt gewordener Ozean weiß sichtlich nicht so recht, was er vom dem halten soll, was ihm da zwischen den Lenden sprießt: eine kleine Frau. Auch sie ist nackt. Solche ironischen Schlenker in der bildenden Kunst interessieren uns herzlich wenig, während wir heranwachsen. Lieber erlesen wir uns die Nacktheit. Im ganz verkehrten Alter gibt man uns Ludwig Tiecks „Runenberg" in die Hand. Mächtig sind die Glieder der Frau, die da nackt im Kristallsaal auf und ab schreitet. Nicht so abschreckend, aber ähnlich fesselnd ist Hebbels Judith. Geht Nacktheit immer so zweischneidig aus? Erster Narzißmus, erste Eitelkeit beruhigen dann wieder. Kein Spiegel ist groß genug. Der Wunsch, sich zu betrachten, bleibt manchem bis ins hohe Alter. Mae West, die statuarische Blondine der dreißiger Jahre, stellte sich das goldschimmernde Wohnzimmer mit nackten Ebenbildern voll. Vor ihr waren schon andere Damen auf dieselbe Idee gekommen. Diane von Poitier und Madame de Pompadour hängten in ihre Salons weibliche Akte, die schmeichelhaft sie selbst darstellten. Eine liebenswerte Torheit, der auch Männer nicht abgeneigt waren. Sie nutzten die Mode des sechzehnten Jahrhunderts, sich als klassische Götter porträtieren zu lassen. Und die waren nackt. Der genuesische Admiral Andrea Doria wollte sich als Neptun sehen. Noch heute entzückt das verrutschte Lendentuch, das einen Schatten blicken läßt. Das ist eine Abwechslung zu dem starken Tobak, den wir inzwischen gewöhnt sind. Schriftlich wie optisch. Es ist sehr schnell gegangen.

Doch wie weit darf man gehen? Kein nackter Mensch erträgt es, lange betrachtet zu werden. Vor allem kein Mann. Psyche betrachtet den schlafenden Amor. Von ihrer Lampe tropft heißes Öl auf seinen Arm. Er erkennt und verschwindet. Bei D. H. Lawrence kommt ein Wildhüter nicht darüber hinweg, daß sich seine Frau an ihm wie an einem griechischen Standbild delektiert hat. Doch auch Goethe ist vorsichtig und zählt der römischen Geliebten „des Hexameters Maß leise mit fingernder Hand" erst dann auf den nackten Rücken, als

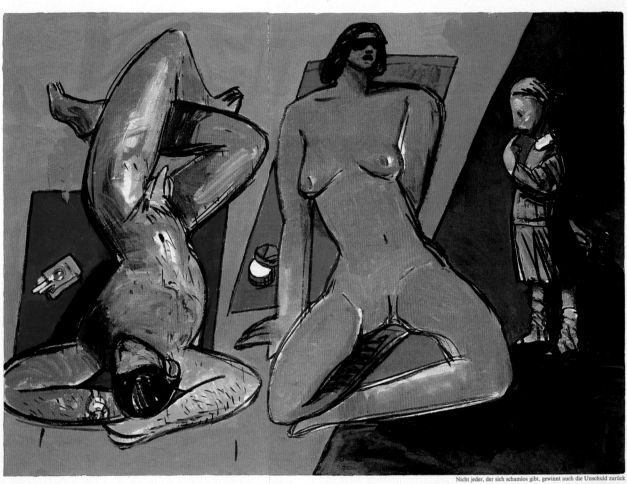

Nicht jeder, der sich schamlos gibt, gewinnt auch die Unschuld zurück

48

Kaffee- oder
Teetrinken ist eine Frage der
Geisteshaltung –
und eine Frage des ästhetischen
Genusses am Geschirr.
Schon die Kannen zeigen deut-
liche Unterschiede

Von Hans Scherer
Illustrationen Heinz Edelmann

TEE, BITTE!

Geborene Teetrinker erkennt man daran, daß ihnen zum Thema Tee nichts einfällt. Da jedoch alle bekannten Teetrinker unentwegt über ihren Tee reden, über Zubereitung, Provenienz, Wirkung, Stimmung, auch über sich selbst natürlich und ihr bemerkenswert eigenwilliges Verhältnis zum Tee, drängt sich dem Beobachter der Gedanke auf, daß es sich hierbei vorwiegend um eifernde Konvertiten handelt, Abkömmlinge gewöhnlicher Kaffeefamilien, deren lautstarkes Bekenntnis zum Tee die Erinnerung an eine private Revolution beschwört. Das eindrucksvollste Teesortiment, das ich je sah, habe ich in der Wohnung eines ehemaligen Alkoholikers entdeckt. Ich weiß nicht, wie viele Sorten der Schrank barg, es müssen vierzig, fünfzig Dosen oder mehr gewesen sein, jede Dose penibel beschriftet, vom Lindenblütentee bis zum Darjeeling, auch Abarten wie Vanille, Apfelblüten, Kirschen und Maracuja, dazu Essenzen, Öle, Tiegel, Töpfe, Zucker in allen Vorkommensarten; der Küchenschrank war zu einer Tee-Orgel geworden, auf der ihr Besitzer virtuos zu spielen verstand. An einem Abend versuchten wir fünf verschiedene, zum Teil abenteuerliche Mischungen, ehe wir zu dem Ergebnis kamen, daß der ungemischte Tee doch der beste sei. Das radikale Umsteigen auf den Tee bedurfte all dieser Rituale, übrigens nicht nur in diesem höchst außergewöhnlichen Falle.

23

Publication
Frankfurter Allgemeine Magazin
Art Director
Hans-Georg Pospischil
Illustration
Heinz Edelmann

DER SCHMERZ

Von Karl Markus Michel
Illustrationen
Heinz Edelmann

Da muß ein Bastler am Werke sein: er klopft und pocht und bohrt; er schneidet, sticht und sägt; er nagt, beißt, reißt und wühlt und brennt. Der Schmerz. Und der Stoff, den er so wütend oder tückisch bearbeitet, sind wir, unser Leib, der, wenn das Werk vollendet ist, als Corpus daliegt, als Leichnam.

Bevor es soweit ist, haben wir Gelegenheit genug, den Schmerz zu studieren, bei anderen und am eigenen Leib. „Gedulde dich", sagt König Lear zu dem geblendeten Gloster. „Du weißt, wenn wir die erste Luft einatmen, / Schrein wir und winseln." Damit ist fast schon alles gesagt. Schreien, winseln, jammern, stöhnen, auch wenn wir keinen Laut von uns geben und selbst noch unsere Mimik beherrschen, von Kindheit an – das ist unsere Sprache des Schmerzes. Eine andere, so scheint es, kennen wir nicht. Wir kennen deshalb den Schmerz nicht. Die Metaphern, mit denen wir seine Arbeit an unserem Leib umschreiben, gleichviel, ob diese „von außen" oder „von innen" geschieht, verlangen nach einem Subjekt: wer bohrt, sticht, beißt? Aber es gibt kein Subjekt, kein Gesicht, keinen Namen, nur die nackte Abstraktion „Schmerz", der dann, in einer anderen Metaphorik, bestimmte Attribute zugelegt werden: scharf und spitz, dumpf und drükkend, anfall- oder krampfartig. Darüber können wir uns eben noch verständigen. Alles andere, von der Stärke des Schmerzes bis zu den Sensationen, die ihn begleiten, entzieht sich der Mitteilung. Oft gelingt nicht einmal eine genaue Lokalisierung; die schmerzende Stelle erscheint übergroß, wir sind nur noch Backe oder Magen, der Rest des Körpers hängt sinnlos daran.

Aber nicht nur anderen können wir nicht sagen, was wir leiden, wir können es uns selbst nicht sagen und deshalb, was ja fast zu begrüßen ist, uns kaum an ausgestandene Schmerzen erinnern. Nur an regelmäßig wiederkehrende Schmerzen erinnern wir uns im einzelnen; und nur wenn wir das, was wir fühlen, sogleich verbalisieren, können wir darüber reden: in einer Privatsprache, einer Privatmythologie. „Sie hatte das Gefühl, daß die Wände sich neigten und auf sie zu stürzen drohten. Sie meinte, daß draußen ein Sturm tobe . . . Dann drängte es sie, ihre Empfindungen zu beschreiben. Stundenlang suchte sie vergeblich nach dem geeigneten Wort. Es sei, sagte sie, seltsam und furchtbar, sie fühle sich wie gefoltert und empfinde doch keine Schmerzen . . ." (Italo Svevo, „Una vita").

„Wie wenn" und „Als ob": In diesem Modus erlebt auch der teilnehmende Beobachter das Leiden: „Die Krankheit, welcher der arme Organismus seiner Mutter erlag, er-

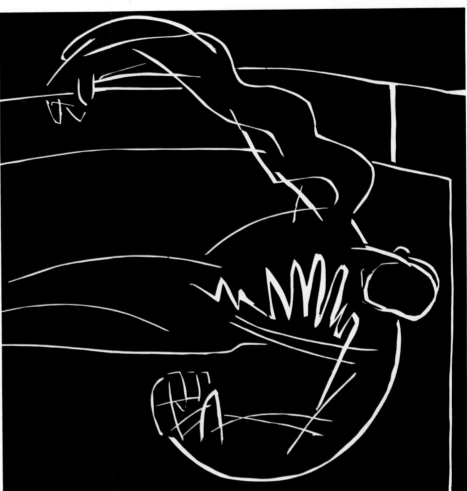

Kommt dir ein Schmerz, so halte still – und frage, was er von dir will: Auch der Gerechte muß leiden

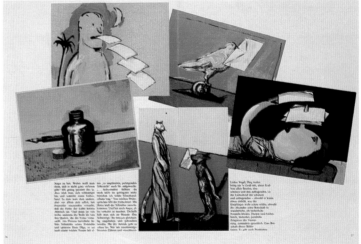

JIMMY LEE UND DER LIEBE GOTT
Fundamentalistische Heilsgaben des amerikanischen TV
Von Martin Kilian

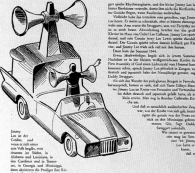

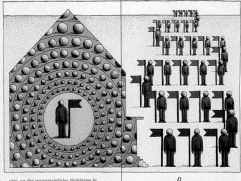

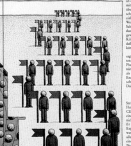

KROKODILWÄCHTER *(Pluvianus aegyptius)* ...

MADENHACKER *(Buphagus africanus)* ...

Publisher
NewMag Verlag
Publication
Trans Atlantik
Senior Editor
Marianne Schmidt
Art Director
Rainer Wörtmann
Designer
Klaus Meyer

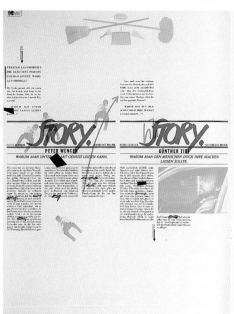
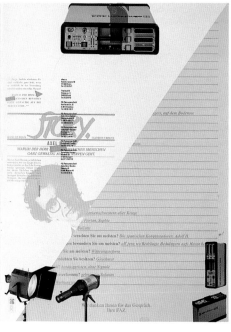

Publication
Auspuff
Senior Editor / Art Director
Urs Schwerzmann
Designer
Ute Vollenweider
Photographer
Dietmar Henneka
Illustration
Urs Schwerzmann

...den Schädel zertrüm-mern. Die Kugel ab-lecken, reinrotzen, mit den Nü-stern an-treiben, sie küssen und kosen: Fußball ist...

...besser als Krieg. Unsere Mannschaft gegen Liby-en. Da, du böser Feind, wir fürchten dich. Wir sind...

...keine brutalen Muskel-protze, die ihre kräfti-gen Ober-schenkel wie Kampf-maschinen gegen See-kühe an-rennen lassen, sondern...

...und Schmutz, Rührei in der Hose, Scheiße aufs Trikot, quäl mich, schlag mich, tritt mich, für das deut-sche Vater-land.

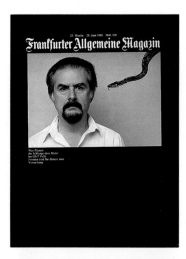

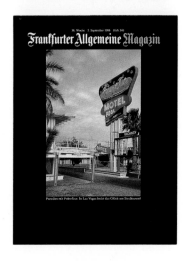

Publication
Tempo
Senior Editor
Markus Peichl
Art Director
Lo Breier
Designers
Dirk Linke,
Judith Grubinger,
Armin Ogris

Publication
FAZ-Magazin
Senior Editor
Thomas Schröder
Art Director
Hans-Georg Pospischil

Publisher
Photo Design & Technik GmbH
Designers
Hans Rüdiger Lutz
Alfred Lutz

Publication
FAZ-Magazin
Art Director
Hans-Georg Pospischil
Photographer
Frank Horvat

Client
Hapag Lloyd AG
Designer
Leonhardt & Kern

Publisher
Photo Design
& Technik GmbH
Designers
Hans Rüdiger Lutz
Alfred Lutz

Publication
FAZ-Magazin
Art Director
Hans-Georg Pospischil

Magazine
Trans Atlantik
Art Director
Rainer Wörtmann
Illustrator
Tomi Ungerer
Designer
Katharina Franz

Magazine
Trans Atlantik
Art Director
Rainer Wörtmann
Illustrator
Andrezei Dudzinski
Designer
Katharina Franz

Magazine
Trans Atlantik
Art Director
Rainer Wörtmann
Designer
Klaus Meyer

Magazine
Trans Atlantik
Art Director
Rainer Wörtmann
Illustrator
Uwe Bremer
Designer
Katharina Franz

Publication
Rolling Stone Magazine
Art director
Fred Woodward
Designer
Debra Bishop
Photographer
Herb Ritts
Lettering
Anita Karl

Publication
Rolling Stone Magazine
Art director
Fred Woodward
Designer
Catherine Gilmore-Barnes
Photographer
Herb Ritts

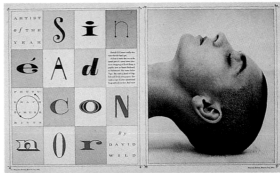

Publication
The New York Times Magazine
Art director
Janet Froelich
Photo Editor
Kathy Ryan
Designer
Kathi Rota
Photographers
Klaus Reisinger, William Coupon

Publication
Life Magazine
Art director
Tom Bentkowski
Designer
Marti Golon
Photographer
Arthur Grace

Publication
Rolling Stone Magazine
Art director / Designer
Fred Woodward
Illustrator
Matt Mahurin

DAS PARADIES DER SCHEINTOTEN

Palm Beach, Florida. Amerikas feinste Adresse. Wer hier lebt, fragt nie, was es kostet, ist im Durchschnitt willkommerscheer, geliftet und über 60. Verändert den Alltag bei der Schönheitspflege, auf der Psychiater-Couch und auf Wohltätigkeitsbällen, den Sonntag am Zunchauer beim Polo. Achtet höchstens noch darauf, bei den »richtigen« Partys gesehen zu werden und so seinen Platz auf der Prestige-Rangliste zu verbessern. Doch ansonsten erlischt das Leben in der greisen Super-reichen in Luxus und Langeweile.

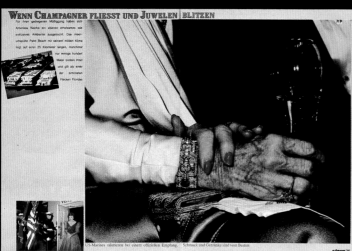

Das »Breakers« mit einer Super-Stretch-Limousine für Gäste; erste Hoteladresse in Palm Beach

WO DER ALTE ADEL MIT DEN NEUEN REICHEN FLIRTET

Standesbluren und gewitztes Geld stößen in Palm Beach nicht zu neuaneordneter Reichtum. Nur bei wenigen Anlässen treffen sich die beiden Gruppen, eines beim »Polo«tschaft«, den die Society feiert, um für die Bedürftigen spenden zu können, um ein Gedeck-preis von tausend Dollar hinzugeben, ein geschmack-vollen Dessert.

Nur der Eismann ist farbig. Unter den Partygästen: Kosmetik-Zarin Estée Lauder (links), Baulöwe Donald Trump und dessen blonde Frau Ivana (Mitte)

WENN CHAMPAGNER FLIESST UND JUWELEN BLITZEN

Für ihren gediegenen Müßiggang haben sich Amerikas Reiche ein ebenso ermahsames wie exklusives Ambiente ausgesucht. Das meer-umspülte Palm Beach mit seinem milden Klima liegt auf einer 25 Kilometer langen, manchmal nur wenige hundert Meter breiten Insel und gilt als einer der schönsten Flecken Floridas.

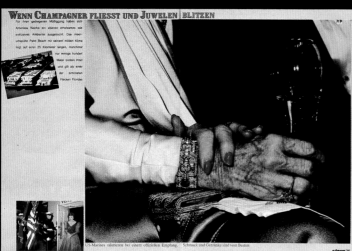

US-Marines salutieren bei einem offiziellen Empfang. Schmuck und Getränke sind vom Besten

ALLES FÜRS PRESTIGE: PORTRAITS, PRUNK KAROSSE, PUDELFRISUREN

Das zentrale Problem der Superreichen von Palm Beach ist, sich von den anderen abzuheben. Da kennt mal schon mal auf ausgefallene Ideen — läßt sich für neues Geld von einem Gesellschaftsmaler auf jung ahncen. Silber-initialen für das Autokennzeichen beschaffen oder im Hunde-Salon »Poodle Paradise« der Liebling rosfarbe anmalen.

Mehrfache Witwe, vielfache Millionärin: Helene Tuch, breiter vor ihrem Lieblings-Portrait

EINE STADT OHNE TELEFONHÄUSCHEN UND TAXIS

Palm Beach ist mit seinen 9700 Einwohnern für US-Verhältnisse ein Nest. Doch ein gutbewachtes: Nirgendwo in den Vereinigten Staaten kommen so viele Polizisten auf einen Einwohner wie hier; stolze Amerikas wie das der Trumps (links) werden extra geschickt. Öffentliche Einrichtungen wie Droschken sind nahezu überflüssig.

Die Müll-Hecke trennst von der Straße: Die Architektur der Villen ist oft so eigenwillig wie die Farbe der Zeitungsautomaten

DER TOD GILT HIER ALS TABU

Alles können sich die Reichen von Palm Beach leisten: Empfänge mit imposanten Prezensionn, einen großen Flughafen mit vielen Privatjets – aber auf einen Friedhof haben sie verzichtet. Wer so taktlos ist, in der Stadt der Millionäre zu sterben, wird im Sarg über die Brücke nach West Palm Beach gefahren und dort begraben.

Ein Bericht von Evelyn Holst mit Fotos von Volker Hinz

S chon um fünf Uhr morgens wölbt sich ein kosmetisch olnwadbleier Himmel über Palm Beach. Die Rolls-Royce und Jaguar schlafen noch in ihren klimatisierten Garagen. Tiefe Ruhe in der Stadt der Millionäre. Dieter Kolbs aber fährt bereits zu dieser frühen Stunde in seinem Firmentaler an der Worth Avenue den feinen Benauchterplatz. Vor ihm liegt sein Werk – das Bild einer schönen, alternden Frau. Genau die Frau, die der Schwenschen Industriedirektion von Ohio verschentte, die ingedann mit einem Foto von sich und einem Zeitungsbild von der 27jährigen Grace Kelly bei ihm erschienen war: »So soll ich aussehen, und zwar bis übermorgen.«

Nachtarbeit für den Portraitfotografen. Stundenlange, knittrige Strichelei, nur weil seine mit der Spe-

Letzte Rast vor der Party-Hast; Beim Diabet-er-Ball gibt's auch echte Ausstellungsstücke aus Europa

REINER
DeROOY

Reiner de Rooy, Tel. 069 706616, Leipziger Straße 59, 6000 Frankfurt 90

Magazine
Instant
Art Directors
Willi Demel
Reinhold Rahm
Designers
Elvira Blazek
Michaela Köhler
Martina Franke
Gabi Rohde

Magazine
Stern Magazin
Art Director
Thomas Höpker
Photographer
Volker Hinz
Designer
Peter Hinze

Calugi e Gianelli

FALCONE
WENSLEICHE 365
SAN PEGRGENESE

898.–

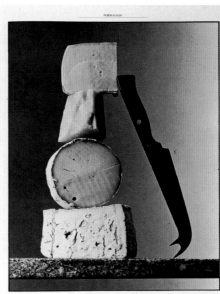

Formaggio Misto

BEL PAESE
PROVOLONE
GORGONZOLA

8.–

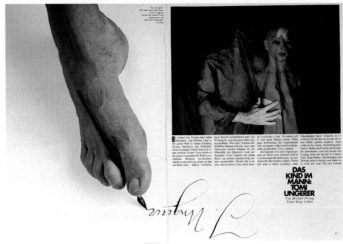

Magazine
FAZ-Magazin
Art Director
Hans-Georg Pospischil
Designer
Bernadette Gotthardt

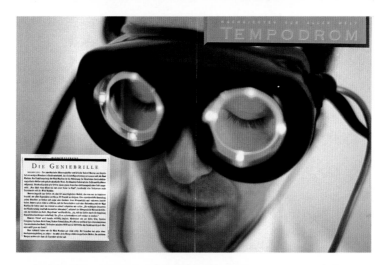

Magazine
Tempo
Art Director
Lo Breier
Designers
Angela Dobrick
Judith Grubinger
Dirk Linke
Photographers
Steve Hughes
Kurt Prasse
Alistair Morrison
Alfred Steffen
Paul von Riel
Paul Schirnhofer
Volker Heinze
Bernd Hoff

Client
Potlatch Corporation
Designers
Kit Hinrichs
Lenore Bartz
Nancy Koc
Photographer
Tom Tracy

Thales of Miletus, one of the fathers of Greek philosophy, founded his school of thought on the premise: "All things are water." Twenty-five hundred years later, nothing has changed in the world to diminish the place and importance of water. It is at the heart of all industries and essential to Potlatch.

Throughout Potlatch's 82-year history, water and the company's successful growth have been inextricably interwoven. In our forests, photosynthesis, the activity that ultimately makes life in the forest and elsewhere possible, would be extremely difficult without the key role played by water.

Rushing rivers in Idaho and Minnesota, and the log drives they sustained for decades, epitomized one of the most colorful and exciting chapters in Potlatch history. Since then, manmade changes in waterways near our operations have helped create major gateways to world markets for Potlatch products.

In early Potlatch mills, steam was used to power lumber saws and waterwheels ran stone pulpwood grinders. Today, huge quantities of water are essential to Potlatch operations throughout the country.

The proper management of this resource in our forests, for transportation, manufacturing or power, and in the environment, remains vitally important to the company's future growth.

Many Potlatch plants were built on rivers or lakes that provided low-cost power, log storage and transportation of supplies and finished goods. Lewiston at the confluence of the Snake and Clearwater, major tributaries of the Columbia; Brainerd on the Mississippi and Cloquet on the St. Louis rivers in northern Minnesota; and Cypress Bend several hundred miles farther south on the Mississippi River in Arkansas, are examples of major Potlatch mill sites that owe their existence to water.

Water

Water is the common denominator of every living thing on earth. Reverently described by some as "Adam's ale," the world's appreciation for this precious resource is boundless. This is our story of how we use and respect water's many qualities in all of our activities.

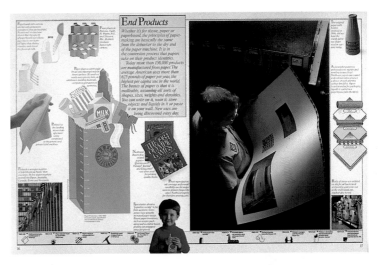

End Products

Whether it's for tissue, paper or paperboard, the principles of papermaking are basically the same: from the debarker to the dry end of the paper machine. It is in the conversion process that papers take on their product identities.

Today more than 150,000 products are manufactured from paper. The average American uses more than 625 pounds of paper per year, the highest per capita use in the world. The beauty of paper is that it is malleable, assuming all sorts of shapes, sizes, weights and densities. You can write on it, wear it, store objects and liquids in it or paste it on your wall. New uses are being discovered every day.

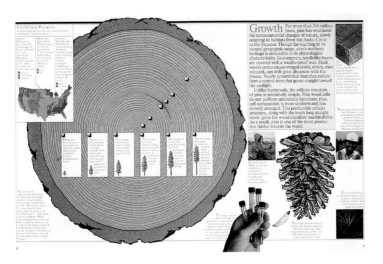

Growth

For more than 300 million years, pine has weathered the temperamental changes of nature, slowly adapting to habitats from the Arctic Circle to the Equator. Though far-reaching in its natural geographic range, pine's northern heritage is noticeable in its physiological characteristics. Its evergreen, needlelike leaves are covered with a weatherproof wax. Hard, woody cones encase winged seeds, which, once released, can drift great distances with the breeze. Nearly symmetrical branches radiate from a central stem that grows straight toward the sunlight.

Unlike hardwoods, the cellular structure of pine is primitively simple. Pine wood cells do not perform specialized functions; thus, cell composition is more uniform and less densely arranged. This predictable cellular structure, along with the tree's long straight trunk, gives the wood excellent machinability. As a result, pine is one of the most productive timber trees in the world.

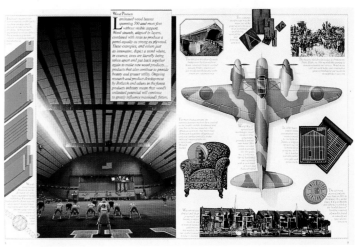

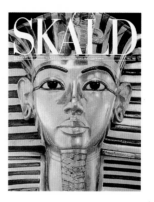

Client
National Medical Enterprises
Designers
Kit Hinrichs
Karen Boone

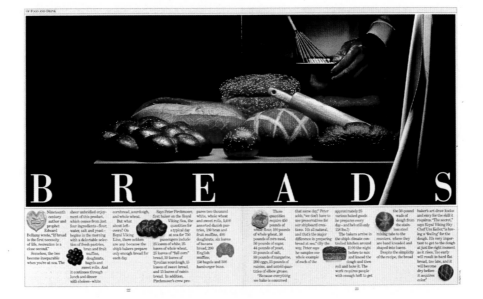

Client
Royal Viking Line
Designers
Kit Hinrichs
Karen Berndt

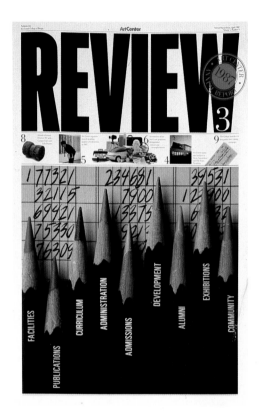

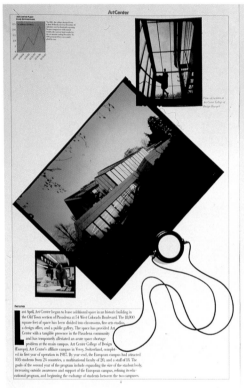

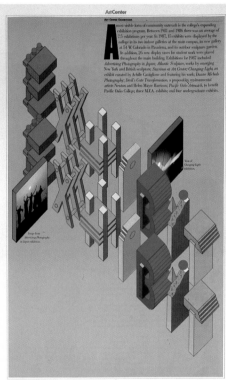

Client
Art Center College of Design
Designer
Kit Hinrichs
Typographic supplier
Spartan Typographers
Studio
Pentragram Design

Client
Art Center College of Design
Designers
(Logo design)
Kit Hinrichs
Cathy Locke
(Reviews)
Kit Hinrichs
Lenore Bartz
Terri Driscoll

HOPE AND GLORY

MATT SCOGGIN
AUSTIN

WILL THESE SEVEN TEXAS ATHLETES SURVIVE THEIR OLYMPIC TRIALS TO BECOME
SEOUL BROTHERS AND SISTERS?   PHOTOGRAPHY BY DON GLENTZER

JESUS GONZALEZ
Bequeno

RAFAEL LORENZANA
Morelos

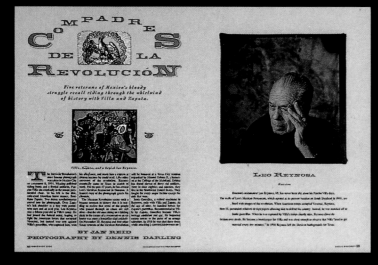

COMPADRES DE LA REVOLUCIÓN

Five veterans of Mexico's bloody struggle recall riding through the whirlwind of history with Villa and Zapata.

LEO REYNOSA
Bastrop

BY JAN REID
PHOTOGRAPHY BY DENNIS DARLING

MIKE ADAMS
SAN ANTONIO

MIKE COLLINS
LA PORTE

Client
Almanac Magazine
Art Director / Designer
Bridget DeSocio
Photographer
George Hurrell
Assistant Art Director
Mary Lou Horvath

Client
Almanac Magazine
Designer
Bridget DeSocio
Photographer
Mark Lyon
Research
Deborah Bell

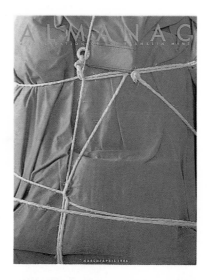

Client / Studio
Texas Monthly
Art Director / Designer
D.J. Stout

Client / Studio
Texas Monthly
Art Director / Designer
D.J. Stout
Photographer
Dennis Darling

Client
Almanac Magazine
Art Directors
Bridget DeSocio
Diane Kobar
Designer
Bridget DeSocio
Photographer
Ted Allen

Client
Almanac Magazine
Art Director / Designer
Bridget DeSocio
Copywriter
Andrew Bill
Illustrator
Raymond Loewy

Spread 1

BY ROBERT SHAROFF
PHOTOGRAPHY BY HANS NELEMAN

Just
WRIGHT

*Thomas Monaghan unveils his unsurpassed
collection of Frank Lloyd Wright decorative objects.*

Spread 2

ORIGINALLY

DEVELOPED

FOR THE

HEARING

IMPAIRED,

CLOSED

CAPTIONING

HAS BECOME

VIDEO'S

LATEST

LEARNING

AID

I READ IT ON TV

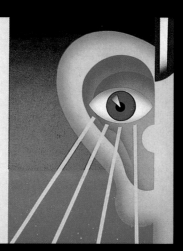

Spread 3

THE SINS OF WALKER RAILEY

*I had to know: did
the minister of the church I grew
up in try to murder
his wife? I told him I thought he
was guilty. "I hear
what you're saying," he said.*

by Lawrence Wright

Spread 4

L E G S
are
B A C K

...And Sometimes They're too Lovely for Words.

Client / Agency
Whittle Communications
Publication
Pursuits
Art Directors
Deborah Hardison
Jonathan Tuttle
Design Director
Bett McClean
Photographer
Hans Neleman
Copywriter
Robert Sharoff

Client
LA Style
Design Director
Michael Brock
Art Director
Marilyn Babcock
Designers
Michael Brock
Marilyn Babcock
Agency
Michael Brock Design

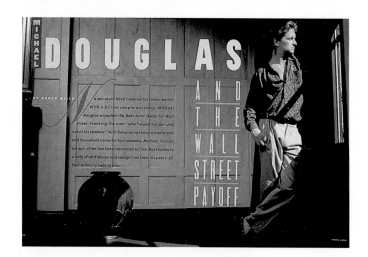

Client
V Magazine
Art Director / Designer
Terry Koppel
Editor
Peter Hauck
Agency
Koppel & Scher

Publication
Sports Illustrated
Art Director
Steven Hoffman
Designers
Steven Hoffman
Darrin Perry
Photographer
Abe Seltzer
Illustrator
Gil Eisner

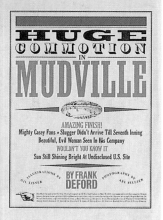

Client / Publication
Texas Monthly
Art Director / Designer
D.J. Stout
Photographer
Geof Kern

Client
V Magazine
Art Director / Designer
Terry Koppel
Editor
Peter Hauck
Agency
Koppel & Scher

Client
V Magazine
Art Director / Designer
Terry Koppel
Photographer
Carolyn Greyshock
Agency
Koppel & Scher

Client
Time Inc.
Publication
Life
Art Director / Designer
Nora Sheehan
Photographer
Abe Frajndlich
Editor
Patricia Ryan
Design
Tom Bentkowski
Director of Photography
Peter Howe

GÖTTLICHES OLYMPIA

HORST P. HORST FOTOGRAFIERT DIE DEUTSCHEN OLYMPIA-STARS

Sie treten in die Arena und werden zu Helden. Sie spannen die Muskeln und gleichen Gott. Der magische Augenblick Olympias, die Stunde der Wahrheit, wie der legendäre Fotograf Horst P. Horst sie sieht. Für TEMPO schickte er die deutschen Olympiasportler auf Zeitreise. Er fotografierte sie als antike Heroen, klassische Athleten und edle Kämpfer. So wünschen wir sie uns auch, wenn am 17. September in Seoul die Olympischen Sommerspiele beginnen.

PRODUKTION: JOCHEN SIEMENS
STYLING: ESTHER WALZ UND PETRA RODECK
HAARE UND MAKE-UP: RICHARD BROCKWELL, ELKE PFLIPS UND
MICHAEL REH

MANFRED NERLINGER

GÖTTLICHES OLYMPIA

Hingegossene Leiber, durchtrainierte Körper, makellose Formen. Sport ist Kunst, Athleten sind Skulpturen. Zu bewundern auf der größten Vernissage der Welt: Olympia.

SVENJA SCHLICHT

ALBIN KILLAT

GÖTTLICHES OLYMPIA

Der baumlange Hochspringer und der gedrungene Ringer, der knochige Marathonläufer und der fleischige Stemmer – Olympia ist eine riesige Freakshow, ein Kuriositätenkabinett begnadeter Körper und gnadenloser Eitelkeit.

CARLO THRÄNHARDT

KLAUS TAFELMEYER

GARY APPEL

DIE STARBOOT- UND SOLING-SEGLER

ROLF DANNENBERG

Magazine
Tempo
Editor in Chief
Markus Peichl
Art Directors
Lo Breier
Walter Schönauer
Designers
Henning Schellhorn
Annette Simons
Angela Dobrick
Copywriter
Jochen Siemens
Photographer
Horst P. Horst

Hommage à Hockney

Für David Hockneys Stil gilt: Die Farben Kaliforniens sind die Farben seiner
Bilder sind die Farben seiner Kleidung. Was letzteres betrifft: Kopieren erlaubt

Magazine
Vogue Men
Editor in Chief
Jürgen Fischer
Art Director
Beda Achermann
Designer
Joachim Peters
Copywriter
Margit J. Mayer
Photographer
Mario Testino

Publication
606 Universl Shelving, Vitsoe
Designer
Neville Brody

Publication
Arena Magazine
Designer
Neville Brody

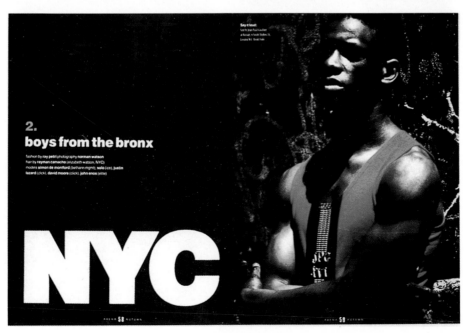

Publication
Arena Magazine
Designer
Neville Brody

PRIVATE VIEW

R O B E R T
E L M S

KNOCK ON WOOD

Publication
Vive, IPC Magazines
Designer
Neville Brody

PARIS

verve

KATHLEEN NOAKS

Publication
The Face
Designer
Neville Brody

Paris

THEY ARE COMING TO BE KNOWN
AS THE *FAST YEARS*: A SOCIAL EXPERIMENT
TO STEER A COUNTRY INTO THE FUTURE...

Photography ANDREW MACPHERSON *Text* PATRICK ZERBIB

Publication
The Face
Designer
Neville Brody

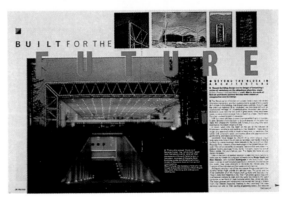

Publication
The Face
Designer
Neville Brody

Client
Marie France
Art Director / Designer
Roland Schenk
Photographer
Roy Volksman

Client
Marie France
Art Director / Designer
Roland Schenk
Photographer
Sacha

Client
Marie France
Art Director / Designer
Roland Schenk
Photographer
Roy Volksman

Client
Marie Claire
Art Director / Designer
Roland Schenk
Photographer
Deborah Turbeville

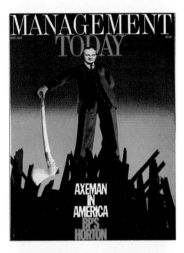

Client
Management Today
Art Director / Designer
Roland Schenk
Photographers
Lawrence Sackman
Phil Jude
Lester Bookbinder
Barney Edwards
Stock Pictures
Phil Jude
Reg Wilkins
John Ellard
Paul Constant
Rolph Gobits
Stuart Redler
Brian Griffin
Illustrators
Gunter Rambow
Peter Brookes
Adrian George

THE LEVITATION OF LEVI STRAUSS

One American firm has become symbolic of the social revolution of the post-war world: the jeans manufacturer, Levi Strauss. Its rise was built on astounding marketing prescience. Norris Willatt

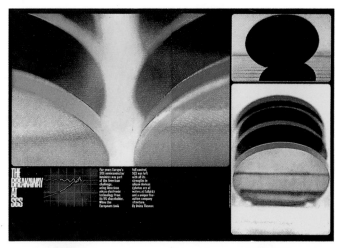

THE BREAKAWAY AT SGS

For years Europe's SGS semiconductor business was part of the American challenge, using American micro-electronic technology from its US shareholder. When the Europeans took full control, SGS was left with all its strengths in silicon devices (photos are of wafers of Falkirk) and a unique five-nation company structure. By Deina Thomas

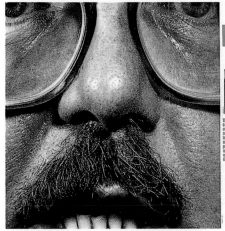

What Watney's Wants

The Watney's horses (above, Mortlake Brewery chestnuts) have a new name: Watney's Red, the climax of years of effort to build up Watney. Mann's marketing, reorganisation and planning. By Deina Thomas

HOW STARS MANAGE THEIR MONEY

While top managers pay top tax rates, pop, film and literary stars contrive to hang on to far more of their income. The new trends in managing the stars' money are examined by Andrew Lumsden

NEW FACE OF TRADE UNIONISM

The GMB, like competitive trade unions, is making an all-out effort to reconstruct its membership, after the union's whole character. Geoffrey Foster

THE MERGER AFTERMATH

One of the favourite industrial sports of the last decade, cheered on by enthusiastic governments, has been the big merger culture left. Sir Humphrey Prideaux, now chairman of Brooke Bond Liebig, came originally from the Liebig side; deputy chairman Laurence Green, right, from the sister company.

But the climate is changing; and the present lull in the proceedings gives a much needed opportunity for both government and industry to take another look at the supposed benefits of concentration and the cult of size. Just one more case of yesterday's wisdom, today's folly? By Simon Caulkin

LAING'S BUILDING BLOCKS

One of the biggest players in the UK construction market, John Laing faces many of the traditional family company problems. But a new strategy to decentralize operations gives managers entrepreneurial incentives. The aim is both to develop exciting divisions and to start new ventures using outside expertise. Will this push enable Laing to break out of the building industry cycle? Annabella Gabb

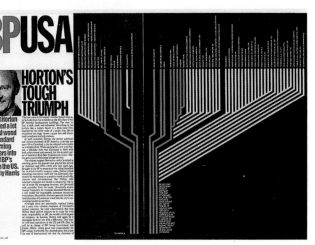

BP USA

HORTON'S TOUGH TRIUMPH

Robert Horton chopped a lot of dead wood off Standard Oil, turning doubters into fans of BP's man in the US. Timothy Harris

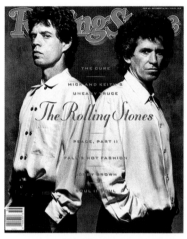

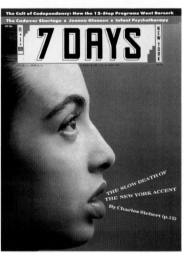

Client
Rolling Stone
Art Director
Fred Woodward
Photographer
Albert Watson

Client
7 Days
Art Director
Scott Menchin
Creative Director / Designer
Scott Menchin
Photographer
William Duke

Client
Rolling Stone
Art Director
Fred Woodward

Client
7 Days
Art Director
Scott Menchin
Creative Director / Designer
Scott Menchin
Photographer
Timothy Greenfield-Sanders

Client
Rolling Stone
Art Director / Designer
Fred Woodward
Photographer
Herb Ritts

Client
Rolling Stone
Art Director
Fred Woodward
Designer
Catherine Gilmore-Barnes
Photographer
Albert Watson

Client
LA Style
Art Director
Michael Brock
Designer
Marilyn Babcock
Photographer
Herb Ritts

Client
Rolling Stone
Art Director
Fred Woodward
Illustrator
Brian Cronin

Client
LA Style
Art Director / Designer
Michael Brock

Client
Premiere
Art Directors
Robert Best
David Walters
Designer
Robert Best
Photographer
Douglas Kirkland

Client
Life Magazine
Art Director
Tom Bentkowski
Designer
Nora Sheehan
Photographer
Timothy White

Client
Texas Monthly
Art Director / Designer
D.J. Stout
Photographer
Sally Gall

CAN PAUL McCARTNEY GET BACK?

He hasn't had a big hit album in years. The other Beatles are suing him. But with *Flowers in the Dirt*, his strong new record, and plans for his first world tour in more than a decade, the ex-Beatle is doing his best to toughen up his image and climb back to the top.

BY JAMES HENKE

SATIS*f*ACTION?

As the Rolling Stones hit the road to support their finest album in a decade, Keith Richards & Mick Jagger work to maintain their delicate truce.

BY DAVID FRICKE

PHOTOGRAPHS BY ALBERT WATSON

PHOTOGRAPHS BY HERB RITTS · PRODUCED BY KATE HARRINGTON

THINLY VEILED

PART TWO: LIVING WITHOUT ENEMIES

Gorbachev wasn't just revolutionizing his own society; he was transforming ours as well. Since Stalin's day, the Soviets had played the perfect enemy. The evil Russian bear defined our national purpose and gave us a global mission. But here was Gorbachev declaring peace. Could we look at him and still see the face of the enemy? And what posed the greater threat, having an enemy or not having one? BY LAWRENCE WRIGHT

PEACE

ILLUSTRATIONS BY BRIAN CRONIN

UNCONVENTIONAL LA PERSPECTIVES

THE RELUCTANT STAR

HOW IN HIS SECOND JAMES BOND FILM, TIMOTHY DALTON MAY FINALLY BE DEALING WITH THE DOUBLE-EDGED SWORD OF STARDOM.

"IT'S TOWARD THE CLIMAX OF THE MOVIE, AND A PETROL TANKER IS EXPLODING," TIMOTHY DALTON IS SAYING. "I'M SUPPOSED TO BE RUNNING AWAY FROM IT. I'LL PREFACE THIS BY SAYING THESE THINGS ARE VERY STRICTLY AND CAREFULLY CONTROLLED." DALTON PAUSES. "WE KNOW IT'S GOING TO BE A BIG BANG,

BY DIANE K. SHAH

BUT NOBODY, NOBODY KNOWS HOW BIG IT'S GOING TO BE. I'M SUPPOSED TO BE WOUNDED AND STAGGERING AWAY FROM IT TOWARD THE CAMERA— THE CAMERA'S ABOUT A HUNDRED YARDS AWAY. EVERYBODY IN THE UNIT HAS TURNED UP TO WATCH THIS MAJOR MOMENT, THIS BIG EXPLOSION, BECAUSE

1939 ★ 1989

Hollywood, the neighborhood, is looking a bit down these days, but Hollywood, the industry, is doing just fine—as are some of the biggest names from the best year ever. At LIFE's request, six stars of 1939 posed with a 1989 actor they admire. The brief encounters occurred in a variety of places. Olivia de Havilland flew into New York from Paris to join William Hurt. James Stewart and Tom Hanks were virtually next-door neighbors in Los Angeles. James Woods traveled to Ginger Rogers's home in Rancho Mirage. These meetings of screen legends and stars who rose to fame during the '80s raise an intriguing question: Mickey Rooney, now 68, just finished *Erik the Viking*; Bette Davis, 81, is in *Wicked Stepmother*; Don Ameche, 80, recently headlined in *Cocoon: The Return* and *Things Change*. Will any of our 1989 stars still be making movies 50 years from now?

ROONEY & KEATON

BATHING BEAUTY

THIS SUMMER'S SWIMSUITS LOOK BACK TO AN AGE OF CLASSIC DESIGN AND SENSUALITY.

PHOTOGRAPHY BY SALLY GALL

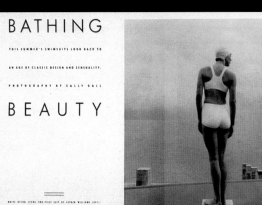

WHITE NYLON LYCRA TWO-PIECE SUIT BY ALFRED WILLIAMS (SAF)

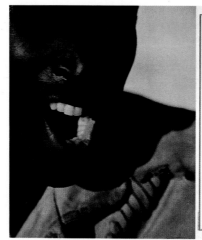

Client
Rolling Stone
Typography / Designer
Angela Skouras
Letterer
Anita Karl

Client
Rolling Stone
Typographer / Designer
Fred Woodward

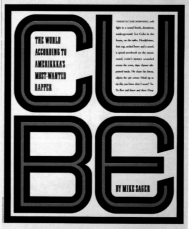

Client
Rolling Stone
Agency
In-House
Typography / Designer
Gail Anderson
Letterer
Dennis Ortiz-Lopez

Client
Rolling Stone
Typography / Designer
Fred Woodward
Letterer
Dennis Ortiz-Lopez

Client ▷
Rolling Stone
Typography / Designer
Fred Woodward
Letterer
Dennis Ortiz-Lopez

SIN
EAD

After weathering some hard and harrowing losses, ***Sinéad***

O'CON
NOR

O'Connor has emerged as the decade's first new superstar

LISA FONSSAGRIVES

"I loved her when I first set eyes on her. We have been married for forty years. Each day is an enrichment."

SUZANNE FARRELL

"She is part real part apparition. I feared that film was not sensitive enough to record my enchantment. I understood Balanchine's obsession with her."

COLETTE

"She lay propped up by a window in the Palais Royal. Near the end of life she was still seductive. To lean my camera onto the bed I moved her small bare feet to one side. I saw that her toes were perfectly painted."

I.P.

(top left, centre)
Client
Rolling Stone
Art Director
Fred Woodward
Typographer / Designer
Debra Bishop
Letterer
Anita Karl

(top right)
Client
Rolling Stone
Art Director
Fred Woodward
Typographer / Designer
Gail Anderson
Letterer
Dennis Ortiz-Lopez

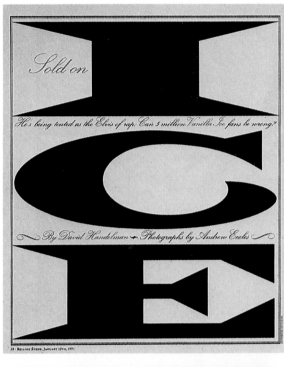

(bottom left)
Client
Rolling Stone
Art Director
Fred Woodward
Typographer / Designer
Angela Skouras
Letterer
Dennis Ortiz-Lopez

◁ *Client*
Allure/Condé Nast Publications
Typographer / Designer
Lucy Sisman
Calligrapher
Irving Penn

(bottom right)
Client
Rolling Stone
Typographer / Designer / Art Director
Fred Woodward
Letterer
Jonathan Hoefler

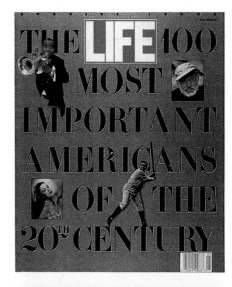

Publication
Life Magazine
Art Director / Designer
Nora Sheehan

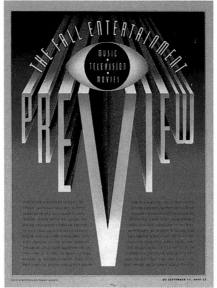

Publication
US Magazine
Art Director
Jolene Cuyler
Designer
Mark W. Shafer
Photographer
Frank W. Ockenfels III

Client
Bull HN Information
Agency
Redgate Communications
Art Director / Creative Director
Gary Koepke

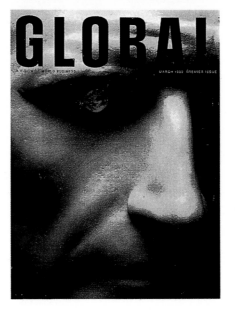

Publication▷
Texas Monthly
Art Director / Designer
Fred Woodward
Photographer
Jim Myers
Lettering
Janice Van Mecham

Publication▷
Texas Monthly
Designer
Fred Woodward
Photographer
M.K. Simque

CHILLY SCENES OF DINNER

Back in the old days, TV dinners were the domain of the listless and the forlorn—silent reminders that your company and your cooking weren't worth a hill of beans

AMERICANS SPEND $26 BILLION A year on frozen food. Our freezers are filled with everything from fish sticks to Häagen-Dazs, and we're cramming more into them every year. Grocery stores across the country are dismantling outdated canned-goods shelves and making room for new refrigerated sections to accommodate the proliferation of frozen products. This is no time to invest in pork 'n' beans, unless you're a survivalist, because we are about to enter the golden age of the TV dinner. Well . . . *I'm* not. I've already entered it and left for good, after eating dozens of frozen dinners so I could separate the palatable from the bad from the completely inedible. Now you won't have to suffer like I did—just refer to my handy dining guide before you take a chance with any TV dinners.

You'll probably be happy to hear that TV dinners as we used to know them are slowly becoming extinct. Swanson introduced the first one in 1952—for $1.09 you got sliced turkey on cornbread, buttered peas, sweet potatoes, and gravy—and they didn't really evolve much over the years. They came in compartmentalized aluminum trays covered with aluminum foil, and they had a reputation for being, well, garbage food. TV dinners were what husbands ate

BY DAVID SEELEY

Photography by Jim Myers, Styling by Jan Thomas, Letterform by Junko Ashitani

---

When the temperature climbs, M. K. Simqu heads for the swimming pools and lakes around Dallas, or anywhere people are trying to escape the heat. What intrigues her about watching people in water is the ambiguity—how water can be supportive and frightening, how it can make people seem almost embryonic. Using a camera manufactured in Hong Kong and marketed as a toy, she has captured the quality of what it is to be hot in summer.

HOT COVER

People think you're hot if you're on TV. I don't even have a TV, really. I've seen, like, two episodes of my own show. To me, hot means uncompromising. It means nonconforming, not afraid, just be what you are and what you feel. I think if you're gonna go for it, you might as well go for it. What else? Oh, yeah—hot is also someone who has nice lips. ~ LISA BONET

PHOTOGRAPH BY MATTHEW ROLSTON

Publication
Rolling Stone
Art Director / Designer
Fred Woodward
Photo Editor
Laurie Kratochvil
Photographer
Matthew Rolston

THE ROLLING STONE INTERVIEW BY DAVID BRESKIN

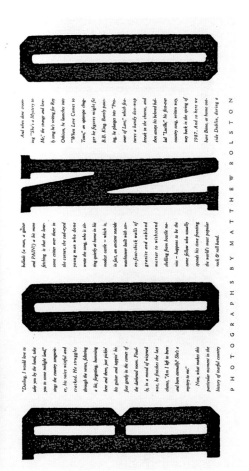

"Darling, I would love to take you to her hand, take you to some twilight land," you to some twilight land," sings the country songwriter, his voice wistful and cracked. He struggles through the verses, faltering a bit, forgetting, humming here and there, just pickin' his guitar and tappin' his foot gently in the corner of the darkened room. Finally, in a mood of wizened woe, he finishes the last chorus, "Am I left to born and born eternally? She's a mystery to me."

Now, what makes this particular moment in the history of tearful country ballads (a man, a guitar and PAIN!) at her some fetching is that the lanesome critter over there in the corner, the sad-eyed young man who has done wrote the song, who is sitting quietly at home in his modest castle – which is, in fact, an ancient stanide warehouse built with seven-foot-thick walls of granite and oxblood mortar to withstand shelling from hostile navies – happens to be the same fellow who usually spends his time fronting the world's most popular rock & roll band.

And when done crooning "She's a Mystery to Me," the strange and lonely song he's writing for Roy Orbison, he launches into "When Love Comes to Town," an uptempo chugger he figures might fit B.B. King. Barely pausing, he plunges into "Prisoner of Love," which features a bandy doo-wop break in the chorus, and then attacks his beloved ballad "Lucille," his first-ever country song, written way, way back in the spring of 1987. And so here we have Bono, at home outside Dublin, during a

PHOTOGRAPHS BY MATTHEW ROLSTON

Publication
Rolling Stone
Art Director / Designer
Fred Woodward
Photo Editor
Laurie Kratochvil
Photographer
Matthew Rolston

53

TOM WOLFE

'Sixties youth culture broke down the walls between people of different status'

A S ONE of the chief architects of new journalism, you put such terms as "good old boy," "radical chic" and "the right stuff" into the language. Did you also come up with the term "new journalism"?
No. As far as I can tell, it was created by Pete Hamill. He was going to write an article about Gay Talese, Jimmy Breslin and a few other writers for Nugget, when Seymour Krim was editing it. Remember Nugget? It was a skin magazine that turned into a literary magazine [laughs]. Those things happen to a lot of people. Anyway, I don't know if he ever wrote the piece, but Krim says that Hamill was the first to use the term. I don't know how conceptual he was being, but the phrase stuck.

Who or what influenced you to go in this new direction?
It wasn't just me, although I was there at the founding. I remember watching and reading Talese and Breslin very closely. And what was exciting was technique. It had nothing to do with stating your opinions, which Jimmy does all the time now. In those days it was almost always a third-person scene. And the technical bravura was what stood out. Never did Gay Talese write in the first person. Never was he impressionistic. It was in the third person, written like a short story. There were a few others, but those two were the standouts. It was one of those things that was in the air.

You may have followed their lead, but didn't you also elaborate on the technique and consciously stretch the boundaries of conventional reporting?
I really made a concentrated effort to get in the game. I adapted a lot of things I had run across in graduate school. For example, there were these early experimental Soviet writers like Aleksei Remizov, Boris Pilniak, Andrei Sobol and the Serapion Brothers. One of them, Yevgeni Zamyatin, was best known for We, the book that Orwell's 1984 was based on. From Zamyatin, I got the idea of the oddly punctuated inner thoughts. I began using a lot of exclamation points and dashes and multiple colons. A lot of dots. The idea was, that's the way people think. People don't think in well-formed sentences. Anyway, they were writing about the Russian Revolution with the techniques of the French symbolists, and it was just electrifying. So here was the perfect thing. They were writing about a real event – usually it was fiction, but it was quite realistic. From the outset, I borrowed heavily from them, and that's a pretty funny thing to do when you're writing for the Sunday

supplement of the New York Herald Tribune [laughs].
And then I began to develop my own techniques. One of the things I used, which I now see has spread everywhere, is the historical present – I don't know how I hit upon that – where you just write an entire story, a nonfiction story, in the present tense. Today most serious first novelists write in the present tense – have you noticed? It does give you a wonderful sense of immediacy.

One recent first novelist, Jay McInerney, made a splash by embellishing the immediacy of the historical present with the second-person singular.
The second-person-singular narration was, as far as I know, introduced by Jimmy Cannon, who was a sports columnist for the New York Journal-American. I think it's a dreadful device. But I'm not one to speak, because in ROLLING STONE I introduced the first-person plural as a story-telling device.

The royal "we"?
The animate "we"! When I wrote the series on the astronauts, I used it because I had this miscellany of figures to write about – seventy-two astronauts – and I had to do it very rapidly. And if you use one of these holsey techniques, like second-person singular and first-person plural, you solve the problem of point of view very neatly. And it wasn't bad – well, actually, it was bad, but it was fun to do. Now, even though I made the historical present my trademark at the outset, I find that it's self-parody for me to lean on it. This can happen. Your own inventions can become deflated currency. How can you start another magazine piece with "Madonna sits there fidgeting with a forelock that just won't sit right. She pouts, she pivots on her seat, she gives me a look through tiger-orange lick-on eyelashes and says . . . "? Somehow, you just can't start a story that way anymore. Well, maybe it's a good thing, because then you try other things.

The power of new journalism seemed to lie in the way it blurred the lines between fiction and nonfiction. And now your latest book, The Bonfire of the Vanities, is a novel. Was it an inevitable progression for you? And isn't your first fiction still heavily rooted in nonfiction – a woman à clef?
I certainly always used novelistic techniques, but I also felt that the boundaries between fact and fiction should never be blurred. Nor is the sense of making you wonder whether you're making something that's true or made up. For that reason, in writing a novel –

PHOTOGRAPH BY CHARLES FORD

BRIAN WILSON *by Annie Leibovitz*
NOVEMBER 4TH, 1976

NORMAN MAILER *by Annie Leibovitz*
JANUARY 18TH, 1975

DAVID BOWIE AND WILLIAM BURROUGHS
by Terry O'Neill
FEBRUARY 28TH, 1974

SALVADOR DALI AND ALICE COOPER
by Annie Leibovitz
MAY 10TH, 1973

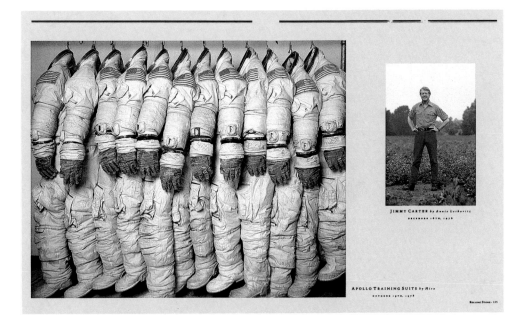

JIMMY CARTER *by Annie Leibovitz*
DECEMBER 16TH, 1976

APOLLO TRAINING SUITS *by Hiro*
OCTOBER 19TH, 1978

ROLLING STONE · 155

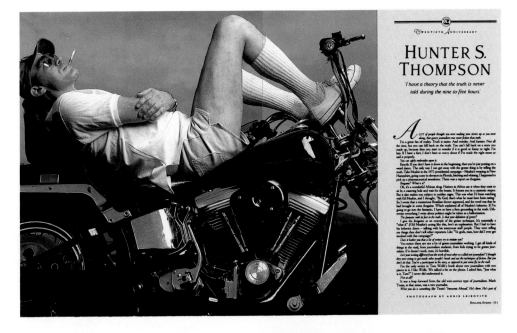

HUNTER S. THOMPSON

'I have a theory that the truth is never told during the nine-to-five hours.'

A LOT of people thought you were making your stories up as you went along, that gonzo journalism was more fiction than truth.

[column of body text]

PHOTOGRAPH BY ANNIE LEIBOVITZ

ROLLING STONE · 231

JACK NICHOLSON

'I still get high. I still like to have a good time with the women. That's not where it's at today.'

PEOPLE lately are very nostalgic for the Sixties. *Do you feel that way?*

[columns of body text]

PHOTOGRAPH BY HERB RITTS

236 · NOVEMBER 7TH–DECEMBER 10TH, 1987

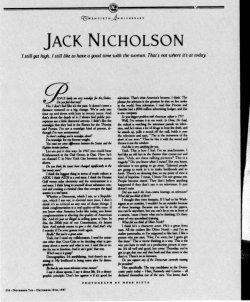

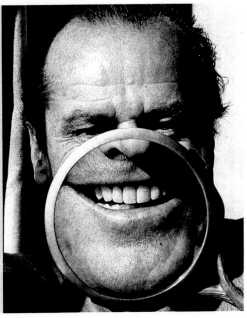

Publication
Rolling Stone
Art Director
Fred Woodward
Designers
Fred Woodward
Jolene Cuyler
Raul Martinez
Photo Editor
Laurie Kratochvil

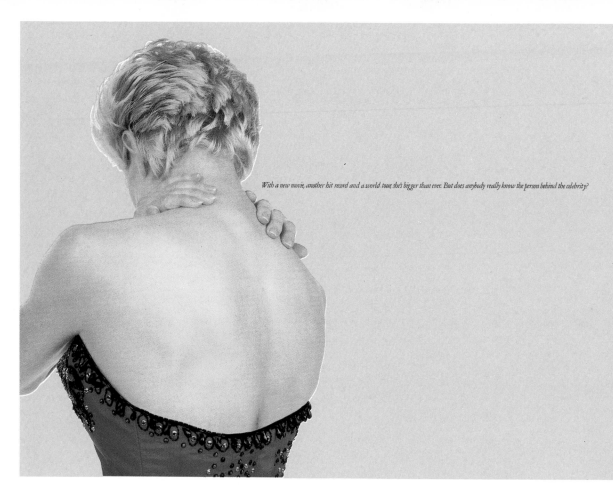

With a new movie, another hit record and a world tour, she's bigger than ever. But does anybody really know the person behind the celebrity?

IT IS A SEVERE, WIND-SWEPT SATURDAY NIGHT IN THE teeming city of Tokyo, and Madonna – the most notorious living blonde in the modern world – sits tucked into the corner of a crowded limousine, glaring at the rain that is lashing steadily against the windows. "We never had to cancel a show before," she says in a low, doleful voice. "Never, never, never." With her upswept hairdo, her cardinal-red lips and her pearly skin, she looks picture perfect lovely – and also utterly glum.

Madonna has come to Japan to launch the biggest pop shebang of the summer, the worldwide Who's That Girl Tour, and since arriving at Narita Airport several days ago, she's been causing an enormous commotion. By all accounts, the twenty-eight-year-old singer, dancer, film star and lollapalooza has been fawned over, feted, followed and photographed more than any visiting pop sensation since the Beatles way back in 1966. All this hubbub is nothing new. In America, Madonna has attracted intense scrutiny throughout her career: from fans, inspired by her alluring manner; from critics, incensed by what they perceive as her vapid tawdriness; and from snoopers of all sorts, curious about the state of her marriage to the gifted and often combative actor Sean Penn. But in Japan – where she enjoys a popularity that has lately eclipsed even that of Michael Jackson and Bruce Springsteen – Madonna is something a bit better than another hot or controversial celebrity: she is an icon of Western fixations.

Tonight, though, Madonna's popularity in the Far

BY MIKAL GILMORE

Let's Get Lost in Cannes

Photographer Bruce Weber caught these moments of unstudied chic in the French seaside town of Cannes, where the operative words in summer fashion are *cool, casual* and *stretch.* Weber was in town to film sequences for *Let's Get Lost,* his upcoming film about the late jazz trumpeter Chet Baker. Directed by Weber and shot by cinematographer Jeff Preiss, the film features vintage footage of the jazzman and cameos by model Lisa Marie, boxer Andy Minsker and actor Rodney Harvey. Weber says he was attracted by the mystique of Cannes, and by the tradition of French cinema: "I fell in love with movies like *Breathless.* I loved the vulnerable attitude in French actors, their movies and personal lives being one. For me, Chet and his music are very much the same."

CHET BAKER

PHOTOGRAPHS BY BRUCE WEBER

F a s h i o n   b y   J o e   M c K e n n a

ROLLING STONE, JUNE 14TH-28TH, 1988

Publication
Rolling Stone
Art Director / Designer
Fred Woodward
Photo Editor
Laurie Kratochvil
Photographer
Herb Ritts

Publication
Rolling Stone
Art Director
Fred Woodward
Designer
Catherine Gilmore-Barnes

Photo Editor
Laurie Kratochvil
Fashion Editor
Joe McKenna
Photographer
Bruce Weber

Publication▷
Rolling Stone Magazine
Art Director
Fred Woodward

CAN TERENCE TRENT D'ARBY BE AS GOOD AS HE THINKS HE IS

BY MIKAL GILMORE

It is three in the morning, and Terence Trent D'Arby — the premier, most provocative pop star of the day — is seated at his dimly lighted hotel room, high above New York City. He is busy studying the floor between his feet, pulling idle at a hammer-and-sickle bauble dangling from his left ear. "I just want to go on record," he says, measuring his time for full effect, "that this is positively the last interview I will ever grant for at least another few years." He pauses for a moment, then looks up and flashes a roguish smile — and for good reason. This is a fairly unexpected overture for such an up-and-coming pop legend — especially considering that this is also the first lengthy interview

PHOTOGRAPHS BY MATTHEW ROLSTON

Publication
Rolling Stone
Art Director
Fred Woodward
Designer
Kathi Rota
Photo Editor
Laurie Kratochvil
Photographer
Matthew Rolston

Imaginary Lennon

The True Story
Behind Albert Goldman's
Character Assassination
of John Lennon

By David Fricke and
Jeffrey Ressner

THE AUGUST 15TH ISSUE OF 'PEOPLE' MAGAZINE HAD BARELY HIT THE newsstands when the calls started coming in. Beatles fans in the Los Angeles area were dazed, confused and hurt by the harrowing tales of drug abuse, violence and anorexia excerpted from Albert Goldman's new biography, *The Lives of John Lennon*. They turned to the dean of the local scene, KROQ-FM DJ Rodney Bingenheimer, for solace.

"I got all these calls at the station," says Bingenheimer, "from kids who were really upset, fifteen-, sixteen-year-old girls who kept asking me, 'Is this really true — is this what John Lennon was really like?' They were really disappointed to read that this was what one of their big heroes was really like."

The truth is that many things are not as they appear in *The Lives of John Lennon*.

The publisher of the book, William Morrow and Company, trumpets Goldman's commercial 719-page tome in the jacket copy as "a startling and revolutionary portrait" of the former Beatle, the exhaustively researched product of six years' work and 1200 interviews conducted around the world. And *The Lives of John Lennon* is certainly nothing if not startling.

The author of similarly iconoclastic biographies of the comedian Lenny Bruce (*Ladies and Gentlemen – Lenny Bruce!!!*) and Elvis Presley (the 1981 best seller *Elvis*), Goldman charges, among other things, that Lennon and Brian Epstein, the manager of the Beatles, had a homosexual relationship until Epstein's death in 1967; that Lennon was a longtime drug addict, even during the "househusband" years at the Dakota, the New York City apartment building where he lived, and that his wife, Yoko Ono, also had a $5000-a-week heroin habit during those years; that Lennon suffered from anorexia and lived an ascetic, Howard Hughes-like existence behind the walls of the Dakota; that Lennon was violent toward his wives, lovers and friends and that he feared he was responsible for the

death of the early Beatle Stu Sutcliffe, having kicked Sutcliffe in the head in a fit of "uncontrollable rage"; and that he was aloof and unloving toward his son Sean.

But an intensive investigation by ROLLING STONE in the weeks following the late-August publication of *The Lives of John Lennon* reveals that it is not, as Morrow claims, "the definitive biography." In fact, the book is riddled with factual inaccuracies, embroidered accounts of true events that border on fiction and suspect information provided by tainted sources. Goldman provides only vague documentation for some of his most serious allegations, and he has drawn considerably from previously published works on Lennon and the Beatles, sometimes without sufficient credit. ROLLING STONE spoke to sources interviewed by Goldman who said that they were misquoted or that the information they provided him was used out of context. Other figures close to Lennon who refused to speak to Goldman or were not contacted by him claim that incidents in the book in which they appear either never happened or did not occur in the way Goldman recounts them.

Two of Goldman's principal sources for life at the Dakota were Fred Seaman, a Lennon-Ono gofer in the late Seventies and early Eighties, and Marnie Hair, a periodic visitor to apartment 72 who lived in the neighborhood. Goldman neglects to say anywhere in his book that in 1983, Seaman pleaded guilty to the theft of some of Lennon's personal effects, including his personal diaries. Nor does he mention that Marnie Hair unsuccessfully sued Ono for $1.5 million in

1982 after claiming that her daughter Caitlin was injured in an accident while visiting Sean at the Lennon vacation home on Long Island.

Harry Nilsson, who was Lennon's drinking partner during the 1973-74 "Lost Weekend" separation from Ono, told ROLLING STONE that Goldman "tried to ply me with alcohol" to get an interview. Tony Monero, who got drunk with Lennon and Nilsson in Greenwich Village one night, produced a tape of his interview with one of Goldman's researchers that shows how Goldman would misrepresent Monero's story with inaccurate and falsified quotations. And Peter Brown, Brian Epstein's personal assistant and an Apple executive following Epstein's death, says that Goldman's lurid description of an attempted rape of Epstein by Lennon and the panic-stricken Beatle's plea to Brown to fly him out of England is "completely untrue." Goldman's main source for the story is Marnie Hair.

Repeated attempts to interview Albert Goldman for this article were unsuccessful. His literary agent, Joan Hawkins, said Goldman was "dubious" about speaking to ROLLING STONE because of the "obvious connection" between the magazine and Lennon and Ono over the years. (In fact, ROLLING STONE published excerpts from Goldman's *Elvis* in 1981.) Defending his work in the September 15th *New York Times*, Goldman admitted that there might be factual errors in his book, but he denied that any had "been made on which a great deal matter – like the interpretation of an episode, or a major point."

Stuart Applebaum, vice-president of publicity at Bantam Books, which is

Publication
Rolling Stone
Art Director / Designer
Fred Woodward
Lettering
Dennis Ortiz-Lopez

THE FOLLOWING EXCERPT IS FROM THE FORTHCOMING THIRD NOVEL IN THE AUTHOR'S BEST-SELLING SERIES OF VAMPIRE CHRONICLES ('INTERVIEW WITH THE VAMPIRE' AND 'THE VAMPIRE LESTAT'). AS THIS PASSAGE BEGINS, THE VAMPIRE KHAYMAN – ONE OF THE OLDEST OF HIS KIND ON EARTH – HAS JUST AWAKENED IN HIS LAIR IN ATHENS, GREECE.

QUEEN OF THE DAMNED
BY ANNE RICE

HIS FACE MUST, AS IF HE HAD BEEN CRYING OR MISERABLY ANXIOUS. He let himself relax slowly. Behold the lamp. The yellow flowers. Nothing. Just Athens with its miles and miles of undistinguished stucco buildings, and the great broken temple of Athena on the hill, looming over all despite the smoke-filled air. Evening time. The divine rush as thousands in their death workaday clothes poured down the escalators to the underground trains. Syntagma Square scattered with the lazy drinkers of ictous or ouzo, suffering beneath the early evening heat. And the little kiosks selling magazines and papers from all lands. He didn't listen to any more of the vampire Lestat's music. He left the American dance halls where they played it.

He moved away from the students who carried small tape players clipped to their belts. Then one night in the heart of the Plaka, with its glaring lights and noisy taverns, he saw other blood drinkers hurrying through the crowds. His heart stopped. Loneliness and fear overcame him. He could not move or speak. Then he tracked them through the steep streets, in and out of one dancing place after another where the electronic music blared. He studied them carefully as they rushed on through the crush of tourists, not aware that he was there. Two males and a female in scant black silk garments, the woman's feet stepped painfully into high-heeled shoes. Silver sunglasses covered their eyes; they whispered together and gave out sudden bursts of laughter; decked with jewels and scent, they flaunted their shining preternatural skin and hair. But never mind these su-

perficial manners; they were very different from him. They were nothing as hard and white, to begin with. In fact they were made up of so much soft human tissue that they were animated corpses still. Beguilingly pink and weak. And how they needed the blood of their victims. Why, they were suffering agonies of thirst right now. And surely this was their first nightfe. Because the blood had to work endlessly on all the soft human tissue. It worked not merely to animate the tissue, but to convert it slowly into something else. As for him, he was all made up of that something else. He had no soft human tissue left. Though he lusted for blood, it was not needed for this conversion. Rather he realized suddenly that the blood merely refreshed him, increased his telepathic powers, his ability to fly, or to travel out of his body, or his prodigious strength. Ah, he understood it! For the nameless powers that worked in all of them, he was now a newly perfected host.

Yes, that was it exactly. And they were younger, that's all. They had merely begun their journey towards that vampiric immortality. Didn't he remember? Well, not actually, but he knew it, that they were fledglings, no more than one-or two-hundred years along the way! That was the dangerous time, when you first tasted real blood in, or the others got you, shut you up, burned you, that sort of thing. Many did not survive those years. And how long ago it had been few him, of the first brood. Why, the amount of time was almost inconceivable! He stopped beside the painted wall of a garden, reaching up to rest his hand on a gnarled branch, letting the cool fleecy green leaves touch his face. He felt himself washed in sadness suddenly, sadness more terrible than fear. He heard someone crying, not here but in his head. Who was it? Stop! Well, he would not hurt them, these tender children! No, he wanted only to know them, to embrace them. After all, we are of the same great family, blood drinkers, you and I! But as he drew nearer, as he sent out his silent yet exuberant greeting, they

PHOTOGRAPH BY MATT MAHURIN

HANDLETTERING BY DANIEL PELAVIN

Publication
Rolling Stone
Art Director
Fred Woodward
Designer
Gail Anderson
Lettering
Daniel Pelavin
Photographer
Matt Mahurin

Debi Thomas, strapped into her white Toyota Supra, speeds toward an ice rink in Denver at nearly eighty miles an hour with the Eurythmics on. With the radio blazing, Thomas, one of the country's brightest hopes for an Olympic gold medal, swallows the last crumbs of her second raspberry Pop-Tart.

In the world of skating, a sport known for cliques and omnipresent mothers, Thomas is an outsider. She is brash and irreverent when everyone else is cracking under pressure before a competition, she tells jokes. Calling the sport "too unpredictable" to bank on, Thomas is the first female champion in thirty years to balance full-time university studies with competition (she is a junior in premed at Stanford, having turned down

BLADERUNNER
BY AMY ENGELER

Dynamo Debi Thomas
is America's most forceful
challenger of East
Germany's defending
gold medalist

Harvard and Princeton). She loathes early-morning practices, a time when most skaters take the ice. She hates to train. Yet almost in spite of herself, she wins.

In 1986, Debi Thomas became the first black world champion in the history of the sport. Her skating was fiery, and her jumps – the most challenging element in competition – were at high, so seem men's. The following year, when Thomas returned as the defender with severe tendinitis in both ankles, she lost the title as graciously as she had won it, causing other skaters to wonder if she just didn't care.

"I used to always quit skating," Thomas says, maneuvering in the passing lane. "I'd say, 'I quit this stupid sport!'"

PHOTOGRAPHS BY MARK SELIGER

72 · Rolling Stone, February 25th, 1988

Publication
Rolling Stone
Art Direction / Designer
Fred Woodward
Photo Editor
James Franco
Photographer
Mark Seliger

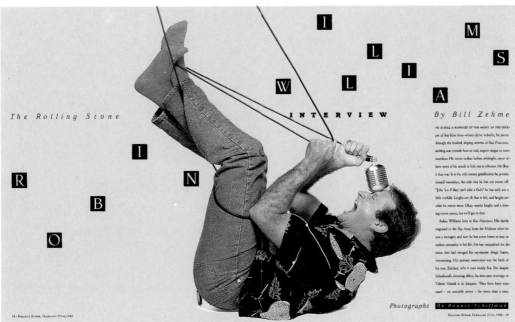

The Rolling Stone INTERVIEW *By Bill Zehme*

ROBIN WILLIAMS

HE IS STILL A RAMPAGE OF THE NIGHT. IN THE COCKpit of his blue blue four-wheel-drive vehicle, he peers through the hushed, sloping arteries of San Francisco, seeking out comrade buzz to raid, improv sieges to commandeer. He never strikes before midnight, never allows word of his attack to leak out in advance. He likes it that way. It is the only instant gratification he permits himself nowadays, the only vice he has not sworn off.

"Joke 'em if they can't take a fuck," he has said, not a little ruefully. Laughs are all that is left, and laughs are what he craves most. Okay, maybe laughs and a thriving movie career, but we'll get to that.

Robin Williams lives in San Francisco. His family migrated to the Bay Area from the Midwest when he was a teenager, and now he has come home to stay, to reclaim normalcy in his life. He has vanquished the demons that had savaged his reputation: drugs, liquor, womanizing. His primary motivation was the birth of his son, Zachary, who is now nearly five. But despite fatherhood's cleansing effect, his nine-year marriage to Valerie Velardi is in disrepair. They have been separated – an amicable arrest – for more than a year,

Photographs By Bonnie Schiffman

78 · Rolling Stone, February 25th, 1988

Rolling Stone, February 25th, 1988 · 79

Publication
Rolling Stone
Art Director
Fred Woodward
Designer
Jolene Cuyler
Photo Editor
James Franco
Photograph
Bonnie Schiffman

MIKHAIL
ARYSHNIKOV
MATTHEW ROLSTON

THE ROLLING STONE INTERVIEW BY NANCY COLLINS

AT THE DELIGHT OF HIS AUDIENCES, BALLET STAR Mikhail Baryshnikov, 39, continues to dazzle, perplex, seduce and, most importantly, produce – prodigiously. His projects this year alone include starring in a movie (*Dancers*, opening October 9th), television productions (Balanchine's *La Sonnambula*, Merce Cunningham's *Duets* and other works), a book (*The Swan Prince*, a picture book that will be published in November by Random) and, of course, dance. In September he will complete his thirty-city tour, *Baryshnikov & Company*, which has been playing to sellout crowds of up to 15,000; on October 5th, he will appear in an AIDS benefit, "Dancing for Life," in New York City. In addition to all of this, he is the artistic director of the American Ballet Theatre, whose season includes a multi-city tour as well as eight weeks at the Metropolitan Opera House, in New York.

It has been thirteen years since the star of the Soviet Union's Kirov Ballet leaped to freedom in the West, taking with him only his memories, including those of a difficult childhood scarred by the death of his mother when he was eleven. Baryshnikov remains single; he has a six-year-old daughter, Alexandra, who lives with her mother, actress Jessica Lange. In Cincinnati, where this interview took place, he was accompanied by Lisa Rinehart, a former ABT ballerina with whom he has reportedly been romantically involved off and on during the past four or five years.

During this part of his tour, his days were passed working the congressional fine-arts hearings. His customary can give him an unexpected openness, al-

Rolling Stone, October 8th, 1987 · 57

Publication
Rolling Stone
Art Director / Designer
Fred Woodward
Photo Editor
Laurie Kratochvil
Photographer
Matthew Rolston

NOTES FROM UNDERGROUND

IN THE SOVIET ECONOMY, IT'S WHAT YOU DON'T SEE THAT COUNTS

G R E E D

ON

the morning that the vodka went on sale, the man with the scarf woke up tired and hurting all over. Eyes full of foam said that he'd tanked up on cheap Russian vodka the night before, the syrupy kind that makes you feel mean and ugly for the next 48 hours. He darted through a convoy of large trucks, his legs sagging like punctured inner tubes, until he found himself a place at the end of a line of 200 men outside an open liquor store in the Moscow of Mikhail Sergevich Gorbachev. The men at the front of the line were working every deal imaginable to get a bottle.

The Soviet premier's yearlong crackdown on the sale and consumption of vodka (it's part of a broad attempt to curtail all income that isn't controlled by the state) has forced the bureaucrats at the Ministry of Food/Vice Ministry of Beer, Mineral Water, Alcoholic Beverages, and Soft Drinks to cut back on the manufacture and sale of distilled potato juice for domestic use, making a flask of vodka more prized than a gallon of wartime gasoline. Vodka is the prime agent of Russian life, a liquid buffer against the harsh realities of life in a police state. Gorbachev made the Soviet Union an almost dry country practically overnight, and the Russian people have been scrambling for the stuff with the zeal of oil brokers in a short market.

Stores that sell wine, beer, and cognac

are open from 2:00 P.M. until 8:00 P.M. on weekdays and from 11:00 A.M. on weekends, but stores that sell vodka are now forbidden to open until 4:00 P.M. Shorter hours, cutbacks in production, and price increases have combined to create a flourishing vodka black market; vodka is sometimes even sold under-the-counter in stores that sell only lighter alcoholic beverages.

There's no reliable or rational price structure in the Russian vodka market. Off-the-shelf vodka sells for 10 rubles ($15) a half liter, but the street price can reach $60, depending upon the demand. Anyone who wants to monopolize the free market needs plenty of rubles, although a dealer who doesn't have the money to buy in large quantities can arrange to borrow the capital, usually in return for selling the vodka at a discount back to the lender.

On this morning in late October, the heavily bundled Russian women shambling past the liquor store to buy vegetables at the nearby produce mall watched the juggling and judging of the vodka market gain momentum. Over the course of a few minutes the 200 people had ballooned to 300, blocking the narrow sidewalk next to Sadovo Samotechnaya. Many of them clenched fistfuls of rubles. The shouting, shoving, and fighting to gain entrance through the store's slender door smacked of the gold action on the COMEX floor. The line was a battle, and the people at the end of it knew they had lost.

By the time the man with the scarf made it to the front of the line, someone

BY A. CRAIG COPETAS

80 REGARDIE'S March 1987

"YO, COMRADE, WANNA BUY LEVIS? MEAT?" IN AN ECONOMY THAT'S STARVED FOR VIRTUALLY EVERYTHING, SOVIET BLACK MARKETEERS SOLD ABOUT $7 BILLION WORTH OF GOODS AND SERVICES LAST YEAR.

ILLUSTRATIONS BY DAVID SHANNON

Publication
Regardie's
Art Director
Fred Woodward
Designer
Jolene Cuyler
Illustrator
David Shannon

L CATION!
L CATION!
L CATION!

The Japanese have set their sights on

Washington real estate · By Harry Jaffe

Japanese tourists have become regular visitors to the capital of the United States. Draped with Nikons and Sony video cameras, they cruise the Mall in air-conditioned coaches and gawk at the nation's monuments elbow to elbow with school kids from Cleveland and retirees from Arizona.

But last summer a bus load of Japanese businessmen toured Washington for a different reason. They had come to buy it.

About 20 potential Japanese investors—each with at least $50 million to spend—took the tour at the invitation of a large American brokerage house in cooperation with a major Japanese bank. Their first stop was the Grand Hotel for a seminar on Washington real estate, followed by lunch at a fish house on Maine Avenue. In the afternoon they drove through downtown and took snapshots of attractive commercial properties. At Tysons Corner they ignored the shops and browsed among the office buildings. A Japanese film crew recorded the shopping trip, which later was broadcast on Japanese television.

"The television crew was a big bonus," says Donald Gelier, a vice president of Cushman & Wakefield, the company that **Just two years ago the** sponsored the outing. "We reached beyond those **Japanese didn't own a** clients on the tour to thousands of potential investors." **nickel's worth of real**

Since last summer's excursion Japanese executives have made regular pilgrimages to Washington. Landauer Associates, a New York-based real estate consulting firm, ushers its clients from building to building in stretch limos. The brokerage house **estate in the DC area. Today they've locked up $250 million worth and zeroed in on new targets in the city and suburbs.**

PHOTOGRAPHY BY JIM MYERS

Publication
Regardie's
Art Director / Designer
Fred Woodward
Photographer
Jim Myers

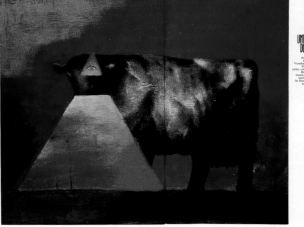

Publisher
FAZ-Magazin
Art Director
Hans-Georg Pospischil
Designers
Peter Breul
Bernadette Gotthardt
Illustrator
Fernando Botero
Photographer
Abe Frajndlich

Publisher
FAZ-Magazin
Art Director
Hans-Georg Pospischil
Designers
Peter Breul
Bernadette Gotthardt
Illustrator
Fernando Botero
Photographer
Abe Frajndlich

Publisher
FAZ-Magazin
Art Director
Hans-Georg Pospischil
Designers
Peter Breul
Bernadette Gotthardt
Illustrator
Fernando Botero
Photographer
Abe Frajndlich

Publisher
FAZ-Magazin
Art Director
Hans-Georg Pospischil
Designers
Peter Breul
Bernadette Gotthardt
Illustrator
Brad Holland

Publisher
FAZ-Magazin
Art Director
Hans-Georg Pospischil
Designers
Peter Breul
Bernadette Gotthardt
Illustrator
Brad Holland

Publisher
FAZ-Magazin
Art Director
Hans-Georg Pospischil
Designers
Peter Breul
Bernadette Gotthardt
Illustrator
Brad Holland

Publisher
FAZ-Magazin
Art Director
Hans-Georg Pospischil
Creative Director / Designer / Illustrator
Seymour Chwast
Agency
The Push Pin Group

Publisher
FAZ-Magazin
Art Director
Hans-Georg Pospischil
Designers
Peter Breul
Bernadette Gotthardt
Photographer
Jürgen Rohrscheid

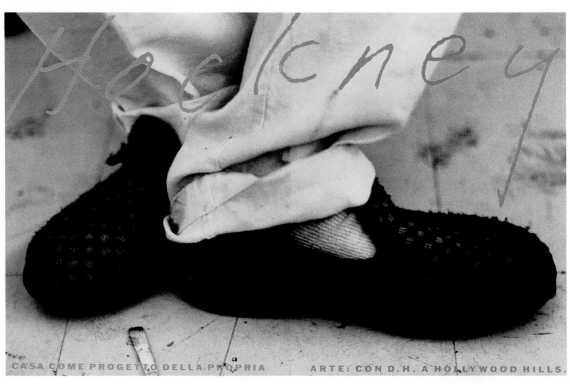

CASA COME PROGETTO DELLA PROPRIA   ARTE: CON D.H. A HOLLYWOOD HILLS.

Publication
Italian Vogue
Art Director
Juan Gatti
Photographer
Javier Vallhonrat

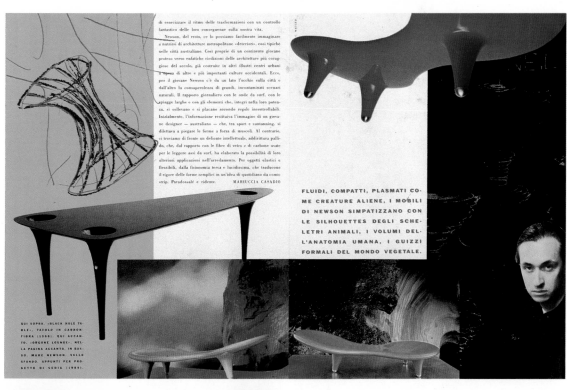

di esercizare il ritmo delle trasformazioni con un controllo fantastico delle loro conseguenze sulla nostra vita.

Newson, del resto, ce lo possiamo facilmente immaginare a nutrirsi di architetture metropolitane «deteriori», così tipiche nelle città australiane. Così proprie di un continente giovane proteso verso enfatiche riedizioni delle architetture più coraggiose del secolo, già costruite in altri illustri centri urbani a opera di altre e più importanti culture occidentali. Ecco, per il giovane Newson c'è da un lato l'occhio sulla città e dall'altro la consapevolezza di grandi, incontaminati scenari naturali. Il rapporto giornaliero con le onde da surf, con le spiagge larghe e con gli elementi che, integri nella loro potenza, si sollevano o si placano secondo regole incontrollabili. Inizialmente, l'informazione restituiva l'immagine di un giovane designer — australiano — che, tra sport e suntanning, si dilettava a piegare le forme a forza di muscoli. Al contrario, ci troviamo di fronte un delicato intellettuale, addirittura pallido, che, dal rapporto con le fibre di vetro e di carbone usate per le leggere assi da surf, ha elaborato la possibilità di loro ulteriori applicazioni nell'arredamento. Per oggetti elastici e flessibili, dalla fisionomia tersa e lucidissima, che traducono il rigore delle forme semplici in un'idea di quotidiano da comic strip. Paradossale e ridente. MARIUCCIA CASADIO

FLUIDI, COMPATTI, PLASMATI COME CREATURE ALIENE, I MOBILI DI NEWSON SIMPATIZZANO CON LE SILHOUETTES DEGLI SCHELETRI ANIMALI, I VOLUMI DELL'ANATOMIA UMANA, I GUIZZI FORMALI DEL MONDO VEGETALE.

QUI SOPRA, «BLACK HOLE TABLE», TAVOLO IN CARBONFIBRA (1988). QUI ACCANTO, «ORGONE LOUNGE», NELLA PAGINA ACCANTO, IN BASSO, MARC NEWSON, SULLO SFONDO, APPUNTI PER PROGETTO DI SEDIA (1989).

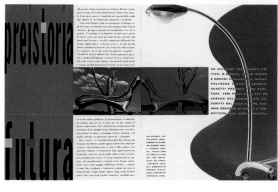

preistoria
futura

UN AVVENTURA TRA SCIENCE FICTION, B-MOVIES, E DESIGN STUDIO E OMAGGIO ALLA NATURA: TAVOLI, POLTRONE E CHAISE LONGUES, OGGETTI PREZIOSI COME SCULTURE, VERI PEZZI UNICI PIÙ UN ARREDO DEL DOMANI. GLI SCRITTI DAL DOMANI, GIOVANE DESIGNER DI STILE E PROGETTISTA DALLA «METAFISICA»...

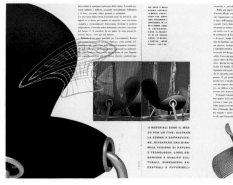

«I MATERIALI SONO IL MEZZO PER UN FINE: AIUTANO LA FORMA A SOPRAVVIVERE. DIVENTANO UNA DINAMICA FUSIONE DI NATURA E TECNOLOGIA, LINEE ORGANICHE E QUALITÀ CULTURALI, DIMENSIONI ANCESTRALI E FUTURIBILI.»

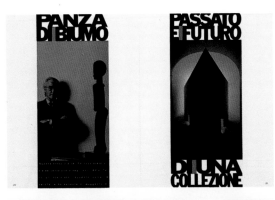

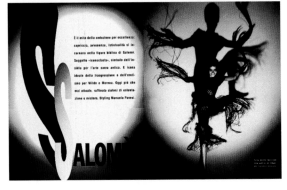

Publication
Vogue Italia
Art Director
Juan Gatti
Photographer
Javier Vallhonrat

CAPPA DI VELLUTO ALAÏA CAPPELLO YOHJI YAMAMOTO

PER DIPINGERE LE «DONNE» HO
RITAGLIATO INIZIALMENTE MOL-
TE BOCCHE. E HO COMINCIATO
PROPRIO PENSANDO CHE TUTTO
DEVE AVERE UNA BOCCA. DIVEN-
TAVA UN PO' COME UN GIOCO
LINGUISTICO. ANZI, IN FONDO
ERA COME UN GIOCO SESSUALE.

Publication
Collectors Magazine
Creative Director / Designer
Larry Vigon

JACQUES · SCHUMACHER
3
BLUE · FANTASY ·

B

RALPH GIBSON

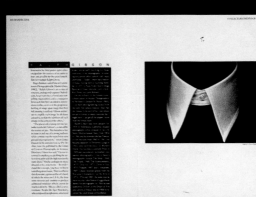

WILLY
Ronis

W

La Casa de Cita

CHRISTIAN

Petra

"During the last three years, I have asked more than 50 women if they would be prepared to create in my studio a sensual image of themselves. They could choose whatever accessories they wanted, and I told them that according to me being sensual did not necessarily mean being nude—no one had to take off their clothes. My only condition, however, was a wooden box—this must somehow appear in each image."

KARIN SZÉKESSY

PART II: THE BLACK-AND-WHITE WORK

Paris Clairoub, 1970

Publication
Collectors Magazine
Designer
Larry Vigon

WORKS IN PROGRESS

LUCIANO TOMASIN

When one looks at Luciano Tomasin's photographs, one is drawn into a universe outside of the ordinary, a surreal, fascinating place. I wonder: Where is this mysterious and disquieting world where women are of a blue so deep that one could drown in them? Where is that planet where le make erogenous zones shine like beacons in the night? Who are these creatures?

To elucidate this mystery for the readers of COLLECTORS PHOTOGRAPHY, I traveled to Padua, a fairly large city in Northern Italy, some twenty miles from Venice. Photographer Luciano Tomasin lives in Padua.

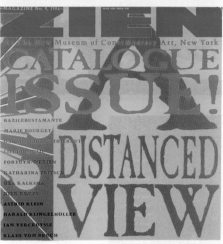

Publication
Zien Magazine
Designer
Gerard Hadders

Hiroshi Sugimoto

White Rhinoceros, 1981

Café des Arts

by Kaap and Klashorst

Peter Nagy

Montemora 9, 1985

Hypnotic Kiss, 1984

Elff Graduate

Zang Tumb Tumb, #465

The Father Size, 1985

Winterthall, 1984

ZANG TUMB TUMB

BAZILEBUSTAMANTE

Ayotea, 1986

"The wise men are seasoned to be
the nine bachelors,
and although they feel
that they ought to be fucking
the woman on top,
they can't make it"

Harlequin
and an improvisation night

Her Adune

The Haunted House, 1987

Stephen De Jaeger

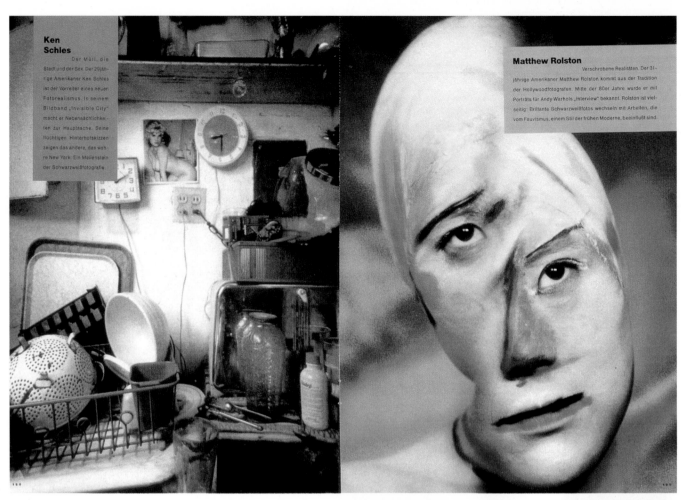

Ken Schles Der Müll, die Stadt und der Sex. Der 29jährige Amerikaner Ken Schles ist der Vorreiter eines neuen Fotorealismus. In seinem Bildband „Invisible City" macht er Nebensächlichkeiten zur Hauptsache. Seine flüchtigen Hinterhofskizzen zeigen das andere, das wahre New York. Ein Meilenstein der Schwarzweißfotografie.

Matthew Rolston Verschrobene Realitäten. Der 31jährige Amerikaner Matthew Rolston kommt aus der Tradition der Hollywoodfotografen. Mitte der 80er Jahre wurde er mit Porträts für Andy Warhols „Interview" bekannt. Rolston ist vielseitig: Brillante Schwarzweißfotos wechseln mit Arbeiten, die vom Fauvismus, einem Stil der frühen Moderne, beeinflußt sind.

schöne aussichten

Kevin Davies Scharfe Schüsse. Der 30jährige Engländer Kevin Davies fackelt nicht lang, sondern drückt ab. Der Ex-Punk haßt technische Spielereien, findet Models albern und verabscheut fashionables Styling. Seine liebsten Inszenierungen sind Trash-Märchen aus der Welt der Sternenkrieger und des High-Tech-Sports.

Brad Branson Double Feature. Der 26jährige Engländer Brad Branson fotografiert kühl, sachlich und distanziert. Seine Hauptarbeit beginnt nach dem Shooting. Im Labor zerstückelt er die Schwarzweißaufnahmen und setzt sie zu surrealen Collagen zusammen. Danach färbt er sie in edlen, dezenten Brauntönen.

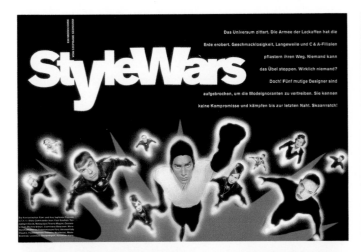

Publication
Tempo
Art Director
Walter Schönauer
Designers
Angela Dobrick
Henning Schellhorn
Dorothee Schweizer
Photographer
Stephane Sednaoui

Publication
Tempo
Art Director
Lo Breier
Designers
Angela Dobrick
Henning Schellhorn
Dorothee Schweizer

Sie wurden aus rassistischen, religiösen,
nationalen, sozialen oder politischen Gründen
verfolgt. Sie sind der Haft, dem Hunger,
der Folter oder dem Krieg entkommen und haben
dabei alles verloren – bis auf ihr Leben.
Auf der ganzen Welt sind zur Zeit mehr als
14 Millionen Menschen auf der

FLUCHT

**Das Leben
im Lager**

**Eine
Notlösung
auf Dauer**

**Sehnsucht
nach einer
Heimat**

**Das Elend
des Hungers**

**Der
allgegen-
wärtige
Tod**

Publication
Stern
Art Director
Wolfgang Behnken
Designer
Bettina Janietz
Photographer
Peter Turnley/Black Star

IN SU BURBIA

ON YER BIKE!

BY JAMES ALLAN

A morning on the road with Auckland's fastest cycle courier.

PHOTOGRAPHS BY JOHN REYNOLDS

Andrew Hubbard...
the fastest legs in town.

LAST COLONY
BY JAN CORBETT

the new-wave cartoonists

Designer
William Chen

GRAPHIS

The International Magazine of Design and Communication

Die internationale Zeitschrift für Design und Kommunikation

Le magazine international du design et de la communication

Specifications:

112 Pages/Seiten

Published bi-monthly
Erscheint alle zwei Monate
Paraît tous les deux mois

Size: 9x12 inches
Format: 23x30 cm

Over 200 color plates
Über 200 Farbbilder
Plus de 200 pages en couleurs

Contents:

The name *Graphis* carries a special meaning that for 50 years has set it apart from all other design magazines. Every other month *Graphis* brings you in-depth profiles on creative leaders in graphic design, illustration, photography, advertising, product design, and architecture and interviews with CEO's of design-directed corporations.

From cover to cover, you'll find an unmatched selection of the best creative talents each field has to offer. Since powerful visions are best evoked through powerful voices, top writers reveal the motivations and inspiration of both past masters and today's luminaries from around the world.

The leading publication of visual communication, *Graphis* is admired internationally by readers who appreciate fine design and designers who appreciate a fine read. Lavishly printed,—*Graphis* will inspire and delight you as it seeks to enlarge the quality of design on every creative front.

For information and prices in US, Canada, Asia and Pacific see the attached subscription order form or call + 1 (212) 532 9387 or fax + 1 (212) 213 3229

GRAPHIS U.S., Inc.
141 Lexington Avenue
New York, NY 10016

For information and prices in Europe, Middle East and Africa see the attached order form or call + 41 (1) 383 8211 or fax + 41 (1) 383 1643

GRAPHIS Press Corp.
Dufourstrasse 107
CH-8008 Zürich, Switzerland

Inhalt:

Graphis ist seit 50 Jahren ein Begriff und hebt sich klar von anderen Design-Magazinen ab. Alle zwei Monate bringt Ihnen *Graphis* aufschlussreiche Berichte über die führenden kreativen Köpfe im Bereich des Graphik-Designs, der Illustration, der Photographie, der Werbung, der Produktgestaltung und der Architektur. Interviews mit Geschäftsführern designbewusster Unternehmen informieren über die Standpunkte der Auftraggeber.

Graphis bietet Ihnen von Ausgabe zu Ausgabe eine einmalige Auswahl der besten kreativen Leistungen in den verschiedenen Bereichen. Grosse Visionen – von grossen Stimmen kundgetan. Nur erstklassige Autoren schreiben über Motivation und Inspiration der Meister von gestern, heute und morgen – aus aller Welt. Führend im Bereich der visuellen Kommunikation, geniesst *Graphis*

international grosses Ansehen bei Lesern, die gutes Design fasziniert und bei Designern, die gute Texte schätzen. *Graphis* erscheint in allerbester Druckqualität. Das Ziel ist, in allen Bereichen des Designs hervorragende Qualität zu fördern. Lassen Sie sich von *Graphis* inspirieren und herausfordern, und messen Sie sich und Ihre Arbeit auf internationaler Ebene.

Preisinformation für Amerika, die Pazifikländer und Asien entnehmen Sie bitte der gegenüberliegenden Bestellkarte oder über:
Tel. + 1 212 532 9387 oder
Fax + 1 212 213 3229

GRAPHIS US Inc.
141 Lexington Avenue
New York, NY 10016

Preisinformation für West- und Osteuropa, den Mittleren Osten und Afrika entnehmen Sie bitte der gegenüberliegenden Bestellkarte oder über:
Tel. + 41 1 383 82 11 oder
Fax + 41 1 383 16 43

GRAPHIS Verlag
Dufourstrasse 107
CH-8008 Zürich, Schweiz

Sommaire:

Le nom de *Graphis* est une référence depuis 50 ans. D'emblée, ce magazine a su se distinguer des autres revues de design. Tous les deux mois, *Graphis* vous propose des reportages détaillés sur les meilleurs créatifs dans des domaines aussi variés que le design graphique, l'illustration, la photographie, la publicité, le design de produits et l'architecture. Vous y trouverez également des interviews de directeurs d'entreprises qui ont mis le design au rang de leurs priorités.

Dans chaque numéro, *Graphis* vous offre un choix unique des créations les plus remarquables réalisées dans ces divers secteurs d'activité. Des images exceptionnelles commentées par de grands noms. Vous découvrirez ainsi les motivations et les sources d'inspiration des plus grands créateurs contemporains du monde entier.

Leader dans le secteur de la communication visuelle, le magazine *Graphis* a acquis une réputation internationale auprès de lecteurs qui sont fascinés par l'esthétique du design et de professionnels qui apprécient de bons articles.

N'hésitez plus! Abonnez-vous dès maintenant à *Graphis*. Vous pourrez y puiser à loisir idées et suggestions. Il vous permettra aussi de vous situer par rapport à la concurrence internationale.

Vous trouverez le prix des abonnements pour l'Amérique, le Canada, l'Asie et la région du Pacifique sur la carte de commande de la page opposée. Pour plus d'information téléphonez au:
tél. + 1 212 532 9387
fax. + 1 212 213 3229

GRAPHIS US Inc.
141 Lexington Avenue
New York, NY 10016

Vous trouverez le prix des abonnements pour l'Europe (Est et Ouest), le Moyen-Orient et l'Afrique sur la carte de commande de la page opposée. Pour plus d'information téléphonez au:
tél. + 41 1 383 82 11
fax + 41 1 383 16 43

Editions GRAPHIS
Dufourstrasse 107
CH-8008 Zürich, Suisse

BUSINESS REPLY MAIL
FIRST CLASS PERMIT NO. 2207 NEW YORK NY

POSTAGE WILL BE PAID BY ADDRESSEE

GRAPHIS US INC
141 LEXINGTON AVENUE
NEW YORK NY 10157-1003

GRAPHIS PRESS CORP.
DUFOURSTRASSE 107
CH–8008 ´ZURICH
SWITZERLAND